FISH & SEAFOOD

FROM THE OCEAN TO THE TABLE

This edition published in 2012
LOVE FOOD is an imprint of Parragon Books Ltd

Parragon
Queen Street House
4 Queen Street
Bath BA1 1HE, UK

ISBN: 978-1-4454-8909-4

Printed in China

Photography by Clive Streeter
Home economy by Angela Drake, Teresa Goldfinch and Emma Jane Frost
Illustrations by Coral Mula

Notes for the Reader

This book uses both metric and imperial measurements. Follow the same units of measurement throughout; do not mix metric and imperial. All spoon measurements are level: teaspoons are assumed to be 5 ml, and tablespoons are assumed to be 15 ml. Unless otherwise stated, milk is assumed to be full fat, eggs and individual vegetables are medium, and pepper is freshly ground black pepper. Unless otherwise stated, all root vegetables should be washed and peeled prior to using.

Garnishes, decorations and serving suggestions are all optional and not necessarily included in the recipe ingredients or method.

The times given are an approximate guide only. Preparation times differ according to the techniques used by different people and the cooking times may also vary from those given. Optional ingredients, variations or serving suggestions have not been included in the time calculations.

Recipes using raw or very lightly cooked eggs should be avoided by infants, the elderly, pregnant women, convalescents and anyone suffering from an illness. Pregnant and breastfeeding women are advised to avoid eating peanuts and peanut products. Sufferers from nut allergies should be aware that some of the ready-made ingredients used in the recipes in this book may contain nuts. Always check the packaging before use.

The Marine Conservation Society (MCS) is a UK charity dedicated to protecting our seas, shores and wildlife.
Please join us – visit our website at www.mcsuk.org
Make a difference – choose sustainable seafood www.fishonline.org
Reg Charity No (England and Wales) 1004005
Reg Charity No (Scotland) SC037480
Company Limited by Guarantee (England and Wales) No 2550966
Registered Office: Unit 3, Wolf Business Park, Alton Road, Ross-on-Wye, HR9 5NB
Tel 01989 566017 VAT No 489 1505 17

Picture acknowledgements
The publisher would like to thank the following for permission to reproduce copyright material on the following pages:
Getty Images: 2, 6–7, 8, 13 (bottom), 14–15, 16–17, 24–25, 52–53, 104–105, 140–141, 188–189
Bryce Beukers-Stewart: 9, 10, 11
Peter Richardson: 11, 13 (top)

A 3

FISH & SEAFOOD

Contents

Introduction

An Introduction to the Marine Conservation Society

The Marine Conservation Society (MCS) is the UK charity dedicated to the protection of our seas, shores and the wildlife that depends on them. MCS campaigns for clean seas and beaches, sustainable fisheries, protection of marine life and their habitats, and the sensitive use of our marine resources for future generations.

What MCS does

The coastal and marine environments of the UK are some of the most beautiful in the world, supporting an astonishing diversity of habitats and species, as well as providing vital resources for economic development, food and recreation. However, our coastal habitats are under increasing pressure from development, tourism and climate change, while further offshore, marine habitats and species are threatened by activities associated with fisheries, aggregate extraction and offshore energy developments.

Through education and community involvement – from marine-life surveys to beach cleans and litter surveys – and collaboration, MCS helps to raise awareness of the many threats that face our marine environment and promotes various types of action at individual, industry and government level to ensure that our seas are fit for life and will remain so in the future.

Fishing for the future

Healthy fish stocks are a vital part of the marine ecosystem, and provide protein and livelihoods for billions of people. Globally, fisheries supply over 2.9 billion people with at least 15 per cent of their average protein intake.

Overfishing is a significant and growing threat to marine biodiversity and many fish stocks are widely reported to be in a state of serious decline. As well as reducing stocks and ultimately affecting the livelihoods of those working in the industry, the methods used can also have devastating impacts on habitats and non-target species such as dolphins, marine turtles and birds, as a result of dredging and by-catch.

Annually, over 51.7 metric tonnes – 47% of the seafood destined for dinner tables worldwide – are currently produced by fish farms. Increasing global demand for fish and the limited quantity of wild fish stocks mean that fish-farm production is expected to double by 2030. After Chile and Norway, the UK is the third largest producer of farmed Atlantic salmon.

By raising awareness of the issues surrounding fishing and fish farming and promoting sustainable seafood consumption, MCS aims to encourage more sustainable fisheries management and practices, securing a long-term future for our fisheries and marine environment.

Protection of marine habitats and species

Although the UK's seas support a variety of life as fascinating and colourful as that found anywhere in the world, providing a home for over 8,000 species, we know very little about the marine environment.

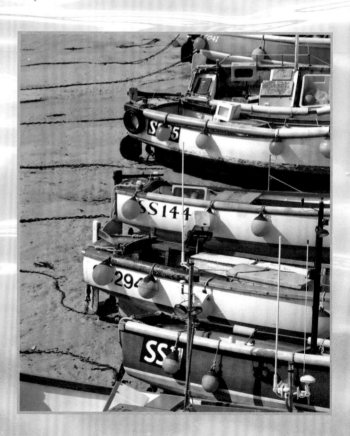

Consequently, protection of marine habitats and species has not kept pace with that of our terrestrial landscapes and wildlife, and our activities are wreaking damage on a significant scale. The MCS Biodiversity Programme uses surveys, education and policy development to ensure that marine species and habitats are afforded protection before it's too late. The programme includes:

- the study of rare yet important species
- campaigning for sanctuaries for marine life – marine reserves – where nothing can be done that would damage marine life. At present only 0.0009% of the UK's seas are protected by two small marine reserves, one at Lundy Island, and one in Lamlash Bay on the Isle of Arran
- campaigning for the introduction of new marine laws to protect marine wildlife and habitats and to ensure the sustainable management of seas and resources
- engaging in vital marine turtle conservation and research and supporting turtle conservation projects around the world.

Pollution-free seas

Toxic chemicals, sewage, crude oil, radioactive waste, agricultural fertilizers, animal waste, storm run-off from our city streets and millions of tonnes of litter all threaten our seas and shoreline. Pollution can contaminate the fish we eat, the water in which we swim and the beaches we visit.

For over 20 years MCS has campaigned in the UK for clean seas and beaches, encouraging everyone to take an active role to prevent further damage.

Community action for clean seas and beaches

Walk along a UK beach and, on average, you'll find 2,000 pieces of litter per kilometre. Beach litter is now a global problem that has a major impact on wildlife, and costs the UK millions of pounds annually in clean-up costs.

MCS has run the Adopt-a-Beach and Beachwatch campaigns since 1993, involving thousands of volunteers in beach cleans and litter surveys every year. It has been able to target specific sources of litter, influence government policy and industry practices, helping to develop solutions to this modern environmental hazard.

The annual MCS *Good Beach Guide* aims to stop the dumping of raw sewage at sea by promoting beaches with the best water quality, recommending beaches that we think are now clean enough for swimming. There's only one charity in the UK that cares for all of our seas, shores and wildlife – MCS. MCS works for sustainable fisheries, clean seas and beaches, protection of marine life and the sensitive use of our marine resources so that they will benefit future generations. Everyone, from individuals to businesses, can support MCS – please go to **www.mcsuk.org** or contact MCS (see page 4 of this book for contact details).

Why Buy Eco-friendly Fish?

Eco-friendly fish is fish that is caught in such a way as to have no harmful effect on the stock, the marine environment or other species. By choosing only fish from healthy, responsibly managed sources, caught using methods that minimize damage to the marine environment and other species, consumers can help drive the market for sustainably produced seafood and make a real difference to the way our fish stocks are managed.

Overfishing and stock depletion

The impact of overfishing on fish stocks and the wider marine environment is an issue of growing global concern. A greater demand for fish as world populations increase and people become aware of the health benefits of eating fish, and other influences such as climate change, are also all contributing to overfishing.

For example, Atlantic cod is listed as a threatened and declining species in the Greater North and Celtic Seas. In the North Sea the stock has declined by 75 per cent since the 1970s. A plan is now in place to allow stocks to recover, although catches must remain low in order for recovery to take place. However, only about 30 per cent of the cod landed by UK vessels into the UK and abroad is caught in the North Sea. Most of the rest of the cod eaten in Britain is imported from areas such as the Barents and Norwegian Seas, where stocks are more sustainably

managed. Landings of haddock, whiting and saithe from the North Sea have all declined since the 1970s and 1980s; indeed, North Sea mackerel has never recovered from the collapse of the fishery in the 1970s and closures remain in place to protect the stock. The common skate, paradoxically, is now becoming very rare in UK shallow seas and in European waters.

The situation in the North Sea, however, has to be balanced with a more positive situation in other UK fisheries, for example in the waters off the southwest coast of England, where there is an increasing understanding of, and a progression towards, more sustainable fisheries.

Impact of fishing on marine species and habitat

Every year hundreds of thousands of marine mammals, turtles and seabirds are killed needlessly in fishing gears all over the world. In many cases these deaths could be avoided, or at least reduced, by introducing the use of 'dolphin-', 'turtle-' and 'seabird-friendly' devices, or by banning the use of damaging practices and by introducing areas in which fishing is prohibited. Similarly, in fisheries where by-catch of seabirds, especially albatross, is problematic, simple practical measures have been devised to help prevent seabirds being hooked and drowned on longlines.

The most widely used and energy-intensive of all fishing methods is trawling. Examples of fishing methods that directly affect the seabed are bottom trawling, beam trawling and dredging. Depending on the nature of the seabed in which these gears are used, the damage to fragile habitats such as cold-water corals and seamounts, can be substantial and irreversible. By restricting their use to areas where the seabed is less sensitive and by adopting measures to reduce the negative impacts associated with them, these fishing methods can be made more sustainable.

Socio-economic consequences

The majority of global catch comes from the waters of developing countries where local inhabitants rely heavily on seafood as a main source of animal protein. As the overfishing crisis in waters of developed countries deepens and demand for fish intensifies, there is increasing pressure on the fishery resources of developing countries. In Europe, for example, a significant proportion of the fish consumed is imported from developing countries. Meanwhile, in the UK, as a result of the industrialization of fisheries and overfishing, the number of fishermen has reduced by 47 per cent in recent years, from 23,990 in 1981 to 12,729 in 2007, leaving once vibrant and bustling harbours lying idle.

Fish farming

Fish farming is often suggested as the solution to the rising demand for fish. Done well it is part of the solution, done badly it is part of the problem. In the UK, marine fish such as salmon and cod are transferred as juveniles from hatcheries to sea pens or cages where they are grown on to harvest size. The pens are suspended in the sea in inshore waters and have a constant flow of water through them. The fish are fed either by hand or by using automated feed systems. All waste and, in some instances, uneaten feed falls through the bottom of the cages to the seabed below. The cages can be damaged during storms or by accidents, which can lead to fish escaping, causing problems for depleted wild salmon stocks as a result of interbreeding and increased competition for food.

MCS Sustainable Seafood Programme

MCS has raised the profile of several important fisheries issues, including 'no take zones' or the introduction of marine reserves to protect fish stocks and habitat, the unsustainability of deep-water fisheries and, most recently, the consumers' role in making environmentally informed choices about the fish they eat, thus increasing support for sustainable fisheries. As the overfishing crisis deepens, the need for the education of consumers to increase demand for responsibly produced seafood has become ever more important.

Fishonline.org

Following the publication of the Good Fish Guide in 2002, MCS launched **www.fishonline.org** in August 2004. The website provides information on over 150 species of fish and shellfish, advice on the status of individual species and/ or stocks and a rating based on their relative sustainability. The website also features a list of Fish to Eat and Fish to Avoid, based on the ratings applied through the Fishonline system. You can also download the most up-to-date version of the MCS Pocket Good Fish Guide, which can be used when out and about, whether eating at a restaurant or fish and chip shop, or doing the weekly shop.

MCS recognizes that many stocks of our favourite fish species are overfished and unsustainable, and appear on our Fish to Avoid list. However, MCS also highlights the stocks of those species that are in a healthier state and provide a more sustainable option. When buying your seafood use the MCS Pocket Good Fish Guide or Fishonline to find the most sustainable option for your favourite seafood.

Increasing the Sustainability
of the Fish You Eat

Consumers can make a real difference to the way our fish stocks are managed. When deciding which fish to eat, consider what it is, where it was caught and how.

Biology and life history

Avoid eating species that are long-lived, slow-growing, late to mature and therefore vulnerable to overfishing. Examples of these types of fish include orange roughy, sharks, skates and some species of ray.

Seasonality

Avoid eating fish during their breeding season. Details of when fish breed are available at the MCS website **www.fishonline.org**.

Size and maturity

Size matters! Avoid eating immature, small, undersized fish and shellfish that have not yet had the chance to reproduce or breed. For more information on the size at which many fish species mature, go to **www.fishonline.org**.

Stock status

Avoid eating fish from depleted stocks. When buying fish you need to be aware that, while certain species are overfished in one area, the situation may not be as bad in another, for example haddock (overfished in the West of Scotland and Faroe Islands but sustainable from the Northeast Arctic).

Fishing method

Where possible, choose the most selective or sustainable fishing method available. When choosing haddock for example, which is generally fished together with cod, whiting and saithe, choose line-caught fish as this reduces the number of cod taken as by-catch. This is especially important where the cod stock is depleted.

Know what you are eating

Often fish is labelled with the generic or family name for the species, for example tuna. There are seven commercially available species of tuna, three of which are listed by World Conservation Union (IUCN). Big-eye has been assessed as vulnerable; Northern bluefin as endangered in the East Atlantic and critically endangered in the West Atlantic and is also listed by Oslo/Paris Convention (OSPAR) as a threatened and declining species; and Southern bluefin is assessed as critically endangered. Also yellowfin tuna is listed as 'least concern' and albacore is listed as 'vulnerable' in the North Atlantic and 'critically endangered' in the South Atlantic.

Look at the label

Look for seafood products bearing the Marine Stewardship Council (MSC) label – The Fish with the Blue Tick. The role of the MSC is to recognize well managed fisheries, via a certification programme, and to harness consumer purchasing power to promote environmentally responsible fisheries. See **www.msc.org** for information.

Farmed fish

When eating farmed fish such as trout, carp and warm-water prawns, look out for the organic label. Scottish rope-grown mussels are a good choice as the methods used in their production have little environmental impact.

US-farmed catfish are also a good choice in terms of sustainability, as they are farmed in closed inland ponds using re-circulating freshwater, both of which processes prevent escapes and disease transfer. Catfish are also fed a primarily vegetarian diet, which reduces pressure on wild fish caught for fish-feed production.

Lobsters, while not farmed, can be ranched or enhanced. In Cornwall, the National Lobster Hatchery at Padstow releases 5–10,000 juvenile lobsters each year to boost wild stocks and to maintain a sustainable fishery for this species. Tagging or V-notching schemes have also been adopted on a regional basis to protect egg-bearing female lobsters. V-notching is the removal of a small piece of tail segment from the tail of an egg-bearing or 'berried' lobster which, if caught, is returned to the sea to continue breeding.

Organic

The organic label applies only to farmed seafood, as only the production of farmed fish can be controlled. The main certification body in the UK, the Soil Association, currently certifies a range of species, including salmon and trout, while standards for other species are under development. Other organic seafood products available in the UK, such as warm-water prawns, are certified by other European bodies such as Naturland in Germany.

Organic farming practices meet high environmental standards, including strict limits and restrictions on the use of medicines, chemicals and sea-lice treatments. Feed is sourced sustainably and the number of fish in the cages is generally fewer than on non-organic farms.

Freedom Food certification

Freedom Food is a scheme run by the RSPCA to ensure high welfare standards are implemented and maintained for farmed animals.

A set of standards has been developed for farmed salmon that is based around the Farm Animal Welfare Council's five principles:

- freedom to express normal behaviour
- freedom from fear and distress
- freedom from hunger and malnutrition
- freedom from discomfort and pain
- freedom from injury and disease.

Buying & Storing Fish

Freshness is the all-important factor to consider when buying any seafood that hasn't been preserved for long-term storage. It is vitally important to know how to recognize a fish that is in prime condition and also how to store your purchase once you have got it home.

Buying

Fresh fish is highly perishable so, unless you have access to supplies as they are landed, much of the 'fresh' fish for sale will have been frozen on the fishing vessel and then thawed.

Whether you are buying your seafood at a supermarket's fish counter, from a fishmonger or from a market stall, the display slab should be spotlessly clean and there should be plenty of crushed ice around the seafood. Whole, gutted fish deteriorate less quickly than steaks or fillets, so look for a display that includes these.

Your nose will give you the first indication of what you should or shouldn't buy. Good-quality fish has a fresh, ocean-like aroma. It shouldn't smell 'fishy'. If there is any whiff of ammonia or unpleasantness, don't buy. The odour is caused by bacteria rapidly multiplying as the fish deteriorates.

Whole fish should be firm, not floppy, and the flesh should feel firm and elastic when you press gently. The eyes should be protruding and clear, not sunken or cloudy; any scales should be shiny and tight against the skin; the gills should be clear and bright red, not dull or grey. Fillets and steaks should be cleanly cut and look moist and fresh, with a shiny 'bloom' on the surface and no yellowing or browning.

Never buy packaged fish with damaged packaging. There should not be much air between the fish and the wrapping or any pools of liquid or blood. And, of course, you should check the use-by date.

The term 'shellfish' includes a wide range of specimens – bivalves (clams, mussels, oysters, scallops), crustaceans (crabs, lobsters, prawns) and cephalopods (squid and octopus) – they should all be consumed on the day of purchase.

When clams, mussels and oysters are sold alive, the shells should be tightly closed; if open shells don't snap shut when tapped, they are dead. They should be in a net or porous bag, not a polythene bag. Most scallops are sold shucked, often with the roe attached, but occasionally in the shell. Shrimp and Dublin Bay prawns are often sold frozen, but can also be raw or cooked. It is best to buy them in the shell – look for firm flesh, and avoid any with black spots on the shells (except in the case of large black tiger prawns). Squid and octopus are both sold fresh and frozen – the flesh shouldn't have any brown patches. Both smell foul if not fresh.

Make sure the packaging on sealed, smoked seafood isn't damaged and that the use-by date hasn't expired. If buying loose, it shouldn't have an unpleasant smell or dry edges. If salt cod is still flexible when you buy, wrap it in a damp towel and chill for up to three weeks; if it is rigid, wrap in foil and chill for up to three months. Always check the best-before dates on canned seafood.

Safe storage

Get your purchase home and refrigerated as soon as possible, ideally transporting it in an insulated bag. Remove all packaging and clean the fish with a damp cloth, then wrap it in wet kitchen paper and place on a lipped plate at the bottom of the fridge, at a temperature no higher than 4°C/40°F.

Leave live clams, mussels and oysters in their bag or put them in a dry bowl and cover with wet kitchen paper. Do not put them in a bowl of water or a sealed container,

as they will die. Store oysters in their shells, rounded cup down, to keep them fresh in their juices, covered with a wet cloth or seaweed.

All shellfish should be stored in the bottom of the fridge and cooked or eaten within 12 hours. Fresh fish should also be cooked and eaten on the day of purchase, although most remain edible for another day if properly refrigerated. Oily fish spoils more quickly than white fish.

Refrigerate smoked or marinated seafood as soon as you get it home, and consume within two or three days, or by the use-by date.

Ways to Cook Fish

Unlike other livestock, fish have naturally tender flesh, so they need very little preparation and cooking. Fish can be cooked in several different ways, but the one thing to guard against is overcooking.

The Canadian Cooking Theory, developed some decades ago, advocates cooking fish for 10 minutes per 2.5 cm/ 1 inch at the thickest part for dry-heat methods. This is an easy approach for anyone new to seafood cooking, but many chefs today prefer 8–9 minutes for slightly less well-cooked fish. This is a matter of personal taste, so experiment and know how to tell when fish is cooked as you enjoy it: perfectly cooked fish is opaque with milky white juices and flakes and comes away from the bone easily; undercooked fish resists flaking, is translucent and has clear juices; overcooked fish looks dry and falls apart into thin pieces. Tuna and other meaty fish can be roasted and pan-seared like beef to be served rare, medium or well done.

When you are chargrilling, sautéeing and pan- or stir-frying, start with a well-heated pan or wok, so that the fish develops a crust that will retain internal moisture.

Dry-heat cooking – barbecuing, grilling, chargrilling and roasting

Whole fish, fillets, steaks and kebabs can be cooked by these methods, and oily fish are particularly suited to grilling, barbecuing and chargrilling, because the natural oils they contain baste the flesh. Their full flavours are not overpowered by smoky aromas. Marinate white fish before barbecuing.

Barbecuing and grilling are similar, with the former cooking from the bottom and the latter from the top. In both cases, position the rack about 10 cm/4 inches from the heat. Brush the rack with oil, add the fish and cook until the flesh flakes easily, basting with a marinade or melted butter. Ideally cook the fish without turning; if the surface is browning too quickly, adjust the rack position. Barbecue thin fillets and small fish, such as sardines, in a hinged fish basket.

Chargrilling is a quick way to give fish a barbecue flavour without having to light a barbecue. Heat a cast-iron griddle pan over a high heat, brush the fish with oil and chargrill until seared on one side and cooked through.

Whole fish are particularly delicious when roasted, as the skin and bones preserve the natural flavours. Preheat the oven to 230°C/450°F/Gas Mark 8 and make a few slashes on each side. Rub the fish with oil, put in a roasting pan and roast, uncovered, until the flesh comes away from the bone when tested – the skin becomes crisp, while the flesh remains tenderly moist.

Wet-heat cooking – poaching, steaming and stewing

Fish is excellent poached or steamed. Although these techniques are very easy, they can still overcook fish so pay close attention. Another advantage is that the cooking liquid can be incorporated into a tasty sauce to serve alongside. Poach in gently simmering liquid flavoured with lemon and herbs for 8–12 minutes per 2.5 cm/1 inch of thickness. When steaming, make sure the seasoned fish never actually touches the water. Steam, covered, for 3–5 minutes for fillets and steaks and 8–9 minutes per 2.5 cm/1 inch of thickness for whole fish.

Seafish stews often contain a variety of fish, simmered with other ingredients. To prevent overcooking, add the seafood towards the end, adding the most delicate pieces last – they will take only 2–3 minutes. Don't allow the liquid to boil.

Cooking in oil – sautéeing, stir-frying and pan- and deep-frying

Fish steaks and fillets are most suited to these quick techniques. For sautéeing and pan-frying, heat 5 mm/ 1/4 inch vegetable oil in a hot sauté or frying pan, dust the fish with seasoned flour and fry over medium–high heat for

Above: **Pan-fried Halibut Steaks with Tomato Salsa (see page 130)**

2–3 minutes on each side for thin fillets, and up to 5–6 minutes per side for steaks 2.5 cm/1 inch thick.

Stir-frying is a method of frying using a little oil over a very high heat, usually done in a wok. It is generally considered a healthy way to cook as ingredients retain more of their nutritional values after cooking than with other cooking methods.

Successful deep-frying requires fish to be coated in batter or crumbs and for the oil to be maintained at a steady 180–190°C/350–375°F. If you don't have a deep-fat fryer with a controlled thermostat, use a heavy-based pan and a thermometer: if the temperature is too cool, the fried fish will be soggy; if it is too high, the outside will be overcooked while the centre will be raw. Work in batches to prevent overcrowding and a reduction in the oil's temperature.

Don't fiddle
When searing, chargrilling, grilling and barbecuing, don't be tempted to turn or move the fish around while cooking, as it may stick to the pan or rack and fall apart. Ideally, turn the fish only once during cooking.

Basic Recipes

The recipes in this book provide an unlimited variety of delicious fish meals. Some of the recipes use common basic recipes which are referred to on these pages, or you could use these basic recipes as an addition to a dish of your choice.

Fish Stock

Makes about 1.4 litres/2½ pints

- 900 g–1.3 kg/2–3 lb fish heads, bones and tails, with any large bones cracked and without any gills
- 1.2 litres/2 pints water
- 500 ml/18 fl oz dry white wine
- 1 onion, thinly sliced
- 1 leek, halved, rinsed and chopped
- 1 carrot, peeled and sliced
- 6 fresh flat-leaf parsley sprigs
- 1 bay leaf
- 4 black peppercorns, lightly crushed

Put the fish trimmings, water and wine in a large, heavy-based saucepan over a medium–high heat and slowly bring to the boil, skimming the surface constantly to remove the grey foam.

When the foam stops forming, reduce the heat to low, add the remaining ingredients and leave the stock to simmer for 30 minutes, skimming the surface occasionally if necessary.

Strain the stock and discard the flavouring ingredients. The stock is now ready to use or can be left to cool completely, then chilled for 1 day, as long as it is brought to a full rolling boil before use. Alternatively, it can be frozen for up to 6 months.

Court Bouillon

Makes about 600 ml/1 pint

- 850 ml/1½ pints water
- 850 ml/1½ pints dry white wine
- 3 tbsp white wine vinegar
- 2 large carrots, roughly chopped
- 1 onion, roughly chopped
- 2 celery sticks, roughly chopped
- 2 leeks, roughly chopped
- 2 garlic cloves, roughly chopped
- 2 fresh bay leaves
- 4 fresh parsley sprigs
- 6 black peppercorns
- 1 tsp sea salt

Put all the ingredients into a large saucepan and slowly bring to the boil. Cover and simmer gently for 30 minutes. Strain the liquid through a fine sieve into a clean saucepan. Bring to the boil again and simmer fast, uncovered, for 15–20 minutes, until reduced to 600 ml/1 pint.

Béchamel Sauce

- 300 ml/10 fl oz milk
- 4 cloves
- 1 bay leaf
- pinch of freshly grated nutmeg
- 25 g/1 oz butter or margarine
- 2 tbsp plain flour
- salt and pepper

Put the milk in a saucepan and add the cloves, bay leaf and nutmeg. Gradually bring to the boil. Remove from the heat and set aside for 15 minutes.

Melt the butter in another saucepan and stir in the flour to make a roux. Cook gently, stirring, for 1 minute. Remove the pan from the heat.

Strain the milk and gradually blend into the roux. Return the pan to the heat and gently bring to the boil, stirring, until the sauce thickens. Season to taste with salt and pepper.

Variations

All sorts of ingredients can be added to the basic Béchamel recipe to make interesting sauces that go particularly well with fish.

Watercress Sauce

Add a small bunch of watercress, finely chopped, to the basic sauce.

Parsley Sauce

Add 2 tablespoons of finely chopped fresh parsley to the basic sauce.

Mushroom Sauce

Add 115 g/4 oz finely sliced button mushrooms to the basic sauce with 1 tablespoon of finely chopped fresh tarragon.

Lemon Sauce

Add some finely grated lemon rind and 1 teaspoon of lemon juice to the basic sauce.

Mustard Sauce

Add 1 tablespoon of French mustard and a squeeze of lemon juice to the basic sauce.

Hollandaise Sauce

- 2 tbsp white wine vinegar
- 2 tbsp water
- 6 black peppercorns
- 3 egg yolks
- 250 g/9 oz unsalted butter
- 2 tsp lemon juice
- salt and pepper

Put the vinegar and water into a small saucepan with the peppercorns, bring to the boil, then reduce the heat and simmer until it is reduced to 1 tablespoon (take care, as this happens very quickly). Strain.

Mix the egg yolks in a blender or food processor and add the strained vinegar while the machine is running.

Melt the butter in a small saucepan and heat until it is almost brown. While the blender is running, add three quarters of the butter and the lemon juice, then add the remaining butter and season well with salt and pepper.

Turn the sauce into a serving bowl or keep warm for up to 1 hour in a bowl over a saucepan of warm water. If serving cold, allow to cool and store in the refrigerator for up to 2 days.

Mayonnaise

- 2 egg yolks
- 150 ml/5 fl oz sunflower oil
- 150 ml/5 fl oz olive oil
- 1 tbsp white wine vinegar
- 2 tsp Dijon mustard
- salt and pepper

Beat the egg yolks with a pinch of salt. Combine the oils in a jug. Gradually add one quarter of the oil mixture to the beaten egg, a drop at a time, beating constantly with a whisk or electric mixer.

Beat in the vinegar, then continue adding the combined oils in a steady stream, beating constantly.

Stir in the mustard and season to taste with salt and pepper.

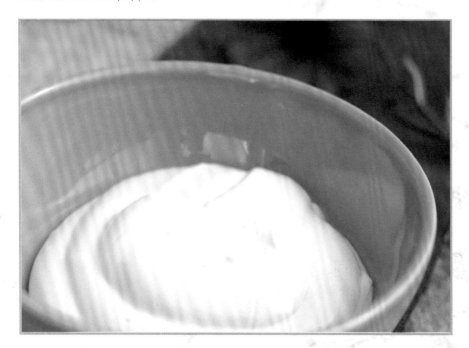

Aïoli

- 1 large egg yolk
- 1 tbsp white wine vinegar or lemon juice
- 2 large garlic cloves, crushed
- 5 tbsp extra virgin olive oil
- 5 tbsp sunflower oil
- salt and pepper

Put the egg yolk, vinegar, garlic, and salt and pepper to taste in a bowl and whisk until all the ingredients are well blended.

Add the olive oil, then the sunflower oil, drop by drop at first, and then, when the sauce begins to thicken, in a slow, steady stream until it is thick and smooth.

Sushi Rice

- 250 g/9 oz sushi rice
- 325 ml/11 fl oz water
- 1 piece of kombu
- 2 tbsp sushi rice seasoning

Wash the sushi rice under cold running water until the water running through it is clear, then drain the rice. Put the rice in a saucepan with the water and the kombu, then cover and bring to the boil as quickly as you can.

Remove the kombu, then reduce the heat and simmer for 10 minutes. Turn off the heat and leave the rice to stand for 15 minutes. Do not take the lid off the saucepan once you have removed the kombu.

Put the hot rice in a large, very shallow bowl and pour the sushi rice seasoning evenly over the surface of the rice. Use one hand to mix the seasoning carefully into the rice with quick cutting strokes using a spatula, and the other to fan the sushi rice in order to cool it quickly.

The sushi rice should look shiny and be at room temperature when you are ready to use it.

Greek Garlic Sauce

- 115 g/4 oz whole blanched almonds
- 3 tbsp fresh white breadcrumbs
- 2 large garlic cloves, crushed
- 2 tsp lemon juice
- 150 ml/5 fl oz extra virgin olive oil
- 4 tbsp hot water
- salt and pepper

Put the almonds in a food processor and blend until finely ground. Add the breadcrumbs, garlic, lemon juice, and salt and pepper to taste, and mix well together. With the machine running, very slowly pour in the oil to form a smooth, thick mixture. When all the oil has been added, blend in the water.

Turn the mixture into a bowl and chill in the refrigerator for at least 2 hours before serving.

Tartare Sauce

- 2 large egg yolks
- 2 tsp Dijon mustard
- 2 tbsp lemon juice or white wine vinegar
- about 300 ml/10 fl oz sunflower oil
- 10 cornichons, finely chopped
- 1 tbsp finely chopped capers
- 1 tbsp finely chopped fresh flat-leaf parsley
- salt
- white pepper

Whiz the egg yolks with the Dijon mustard, and salt and pepper to taste, in a food processor or blender or by hand. Add the lemon juice and whiz again.

With the motor still running or still beating, add the oil, drop by drop at first. When the sauce begins to thicken, the oil can then be added in a slow, steady stream.

Stir in the cornichons, capers and parsley. Taste and adjust the seasoning with extra salt, pepper and lemon juice if necessary. If the sauce seems too thick, slowly add 1 tablespoon of hot water.

Use at once or store in an airtight container in the refrigerator for up to 1 week.

Beurre Blanc

- 3 tbsp very finely chopped shallots
- 2 bay leaves
- 6 black peppercorns, lightly crushed
- 3 tbsp white wine, such as Muscadet
- 3 tbsp white wine vinegar
- 1^1/2 tbsp double cream
- 175 g/6 oz unsalted butter, cut into small pieces
- 2 tsp chopped fresh tarragon
- salt and pepper

Put the shallots, bay leaves, peppercorns, wine and vinegar in a small saucepan over a medium–high heat and boil until reduced to about 1 tablespoon. Strain the mixture through a non-metallic sieve, then return the liquid to the saucepan.

Stir the cream into the liquid and bring to the boil, then reduce the heat to low. Whisk in the butter, piece by piece, not adding the next until the previous one has melted. Whisking constantly and lifting the pan off the heat occasionally will help to prevent the sauce separating. Stir in the tarragon, and salt and pepper to taste, and serve immediately.

Chapter 1
Freshwater Fish

The Freshwater Fish Directory

The following is a guide to all the main species of freshwater fish that can be eaten, listed by their common names, although some fish, confusingly, are known by a variety of different names. The potted profile for each fish details the various forms in which it can be purchased, for example whole or in fillets, fresh or canned, and the most suitable cooking methods.

Catfish

Trout

Eel

Catfish/Rockfish

There are many species of catfish, many of which are sold frozen. It is available whole or as fillets and its tough skin must be removed before cooking. It can be fried, grilled, poached, steamed, baked or used in stews.

Char

Char is similar to trout in size and appearance, but more colourful. Its flesh is firm and usually white, or sometimes pale pink. Arctic char is now commonly available, thanks to farming in Iceland and Canada. It is usually sold filleted and can be fried, baked or steamed.

Eel/Common Eel/Elver

This snake-like fish, smaller than the seawater conger eel, lives in rivers and streams and then swims thousands of kilometres to return to the sea and spawn, after which it

dies (the opposite migratory habit of salmon). Elvers are baby eels and are no longer eaten, but are used to restock fisheries. Eels are currently overfished and should be avoided at the present time.

Tilapia/St Peter's Fish

Farming has made tilapia more widely available and it can now be purchased whole or as fillets. It has a firm texture and is suitable for all cooking methods. An interesting feature of this fish is that the females carry their young in their mouths. They are smaller than the males.

Trout

There are many varieties of trout, including river, brown, rainbow and salmon trout. It is usually cooked whole and can be baked, fried, grilled, poached or steamed. It is also available smoked, in the same way as smoked salmon.

> Preparing a fish noisette from a fish cutlet

1 After removing the pinbones (see page 67), using a sharp knife, remove the skin from the flesh halfway around the cutlet.

2 Curl the skinned piece of fish into the centre and wrap the rest of the cutlet around the outside.

3 Wrap the loose piece of skin around the cutlet and secure the whole noisette with cocktail sticks.

Bacon-wrapped Trout

Serves 4

ingredients
- 4 whole trout, gutted and fins removed, with head left on or removed
- 8 rindless smoked streaky bacon rashers
- 4 tbsp plain flour
- 2 tbsp olive oil
- 2 tbsp lemon juice
- salt and pepper
- salad leaves and lemon wedges, to serve

1 Preheat the grill. Rinse the trout inside and out under cold running water and pat dry with kitchen paper. Stretch the bacon using the back of a heavy flat-bladed knife.

2 Spread the flour out on a large plate and season to taste with salt and pepper. Gently roll each trout in the seasoned flour until well coated, then shake off any excess. Beginning just below the head, wrap two bacon rashers in a spiral along the length of each fish.

3 Brush the trout with the oil and cook under the preheated grill for 10–12 minutes, turning once. Transfer to serving plates and drizzle with the lemon juice. Serve immediately with salad leaves and lemon wedges for squeezing over.

Poached Trout with Beurre Blanc

Serves 4

ingredients
- 4 whole rainbow trout, gutted and fins removed, with head left on or removed
- about 1.2 litres/2 pints court bouillon (see page 20)
- lemon wedges and fresh tarragon sprigs, to garnish
- beurre blanc (see page 23), to serve

1 Rinse the trout inside and out under cold running water and pat dry with kitchen paper.

2 Put the trout in a sauté or frying pan large enough to hold them side by side. Pour over enough court bouillon to cover and slowly bring to the boil. Immediately reduce the heat to very low and leave to simmer for 8–10 minutes, until the flesh flakes easily.

3 Remove the fish from the liquid and pat dry. The fish can now be served whole or skinned and filleted. Transfer to warmed plates, garnish with the lemon wedges and tarragon sprigs, and serve with beurre blanc.

Trout with Mussels & Prawns

Serves 4

ingredients

- 30 g/1 oz butter, plus extra for greasing
- ½ tbsp sunflower oil
- 12 button mushrooms, thinly sliced
- 24 live mussels, scrubbed and debearded
- 1 shallot, chopped
- 1 garlic clove, crushed
- 250 ml/9 fl oz dry white wine
- 24 raw prawns, in their shells
- 4 trout fillets, each about 175 g/ 6 oz, all skin and bones removed
- 250 ml/9 fl oz double cream
- salt and pepper
- fresh chervil sprigs, to garnish

beurre manié

- 15 g/½ oz unsalted butter, softened
- 15 g/½ oz plain flour

1 Melt the butter with the oil in a heavy-based frying pan over a medium–high heat. Add the mushrooms and sauté for 5–7 minutes, until brown, then set aside.

2 Meanwhile, preheat the oven to 190°C/375°F/Gas Mark 5. Lightly grease an ovenproof dish, large enough to hold the trout fillets in a single layer, with butter and set aside.

3 Discard any mussels with broken shells and any that refuse to close when tapped.

4 Put the shallot, garlic and wine in a large saucepan with a tight-fitting lid over a high heat and bring to the boil. Reduce the heat to very low. Add the mussels and prawns to the saucepan, cover tightly and simmer, shaking the pan frequently, for 4 minutes, or until the mussels open and the prawns turn pink. Discard any mussels that remain closed.

5 Line a large sieve with a piece of muslin and place over a large bowl. Tip the contents of the pan into the sieve and strain, reserving the cooking liquid.

6 Remove the mussels from their shells, reserving 4 unshelled mussels for the garnish. Peel the prawns and reserve the shells and heads, then set aside the mussels and prawns.

7 Put the cooking liquid in a small saucepan over a high heat, add the prawn shells and heads, and boil for 3 minutes, skimming the surface if necessary.

8 Lay the trout fillets in the prepared dish and strain over the prawn stock. Scatter over the mushrooms. Cover the dish with foil, shiny side down, and bake in the preheated oven for 10–12 minutes, until the trout is tender and flakes easily. Remove the trout, add to the shellfish and cover to keep warm, reserving the cooking liquid.

9 Meanwhile, to make the beurre manié, mash the butter and flour together to make a thick paste.

10 To make the sauce, pour the cooking liquid into a small saucepan over a high heat. Bring to the boil, then add small amounts of the beurre manié, whisking constantly and adding more only when the previous amount has been incorporated. Continue boiling and whisking until the sauce is thick and shiny. Stir in the cream and boil until the sauce has reduced by half. Season to taste with salt and pepper, then stir in the mussels and prawns and just warm through.

11 Transfer the trout fillets to warmed plates and spoon over the sauce and shellfish. Garnish with the chervil sprigs and the reserved unshelled mussels.

Grilled Trout Stuffed with Mushrooms & Spinach

Serves 2

ingredients

- 2 whole trout, each about 350 g/12 oz, gutted and fins removed
- 1 tbsp vegetable oil
- salt and pepper

stuffing

- 25 g/1 oz butter
- 2 shallots, finely chopped
- 55 g/2 oz mushrooms, finely chopped
- 55 g/2 oz baby spinach
- 1 tbsp chopped fresh parsley or tarragon
- grated rind of 1 lemon
- whole nutmeg, for grating

tomato salsa

- 2 tomatoes, peeled, deseeded and finely diced
- 10-cm/4-inch piece cucumber, finely diced
- 2 spring onions, finely chopped
- 1 tbsp olive oil
- salt and pepper

1 Rinse the trout inside and out under cold running water and pat dry with kitchen paper. Leave the head and tail on and slash the skin of each fish on both sides about 5 times. Brush with the oil and season well with salt and pepper, both inside and out.

2 To make the stuffing, melt the butter in a small saucepan and gently soften the shallots for 2–3 minutes. Add the mushrooms and continue to cook for a further 2 minutes. Add the spinach and heat until it is just wilted. Remove from the heat and add the parsley, lemon rind and a good grating of nutmeg. Allow to cool.

3 Preheat the grill. Fill the cavities of the trout with the mushroom and spinach stuffing, then reshape them as neatly as you can.

4 Cook the trout under the preheated grill for 10–12 minutes, turning once, until cooked through.

5 To make the tomato salsa, mix all the ingredients together and season well with salt and pepper.

6 Serve the trout hot with the tomato salsa spooned over.

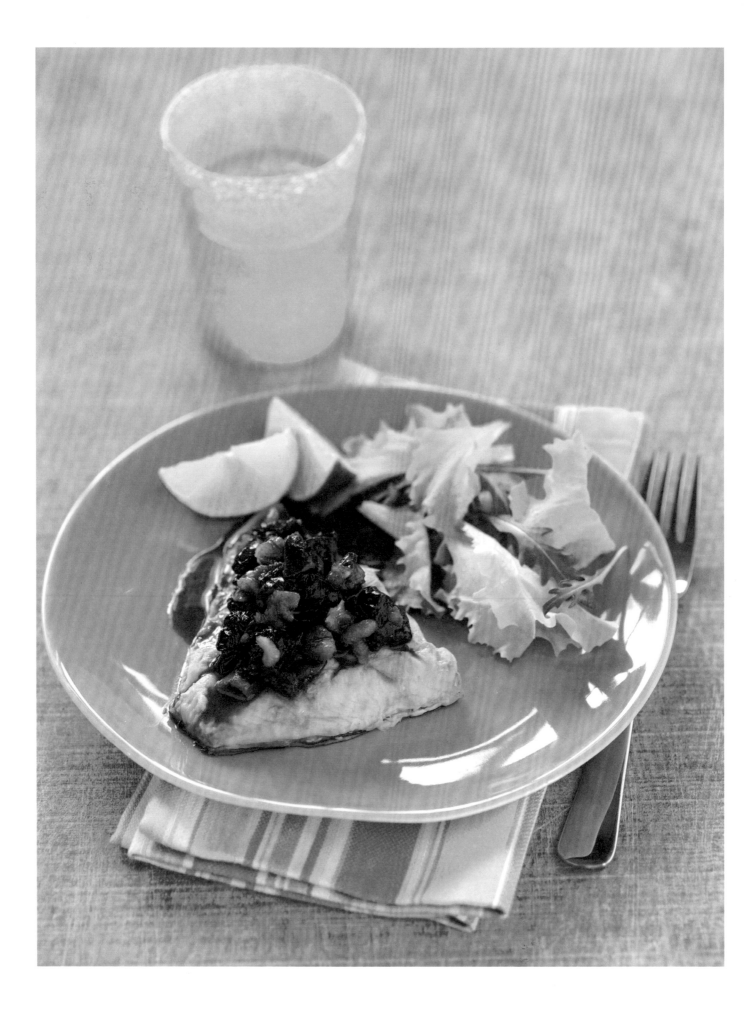

Trout with Dried Fruit Sauce

Serves 6

ingredients

- 6 trout or carp steaks or cutlets, each about 175–225 g/6–8 oz
- 2 onions, sliced
- 1 garlic clove, finely chopped
- 2 celery sticks, sliced
- 1 carrot, chopped
- 1 tsp ground cumin
- 1 tsp ground allspice
- 1 bay leaf
- 6 cloves
- 6 black peppercorns
- 225 ml/8 fl oz white wine vinegar
- 125 ml/4 fl oz beer
- 850 ml/1½ pints water
- 25 g/1 oz butter
- 175 g/6 oz ready-to-eat prunes, chopped
- 55 g/2 oz raisins
- 55 g/2 oz walnuts, finely chopped
- 1 tbsp brown sugar
- grated rind and juice of 1 lemon
- salad leaves and lime wedges, to serve

1 Rinse the fish under cold running water and pat dry with kitchen paper.

2 Put the onions, garlic, celery, carrot, cumin, allspice, bay leaf, cloves and peppercorns in a large saucepan and pour in the vinegar, beer and water. Bring to the boil over a medium heat, then reduce the heat, cover and simmer for 30 minutes.

3 Add the fish to the pan, re-cover and simmer for a further 30 minutes, until the flesh flakes easily.

4 Just before the fish is ready, melt the butter in a saucepan. Stir in the prunes, raisins, walnuts, sugar and lemon rind and juice, and simmer gently.

5 Using a fish slice, transfer the fish to a warmed serving dish and keep warm. Strain the cooking liquid and discard the vegetables and flavouring solids. Measure 450 ml/16 fl oz of the cooking liquid and stir it into the prune and raisin mixture. Cook over a low heat, stirring frequently, for 5 minutes, until heated through. Spoon the sauce over the fish and serve immediately with salad leaves and lime wedges.

Deep-fried River Fish
with Chilli Bean Sauce

Serves 2

ingredients

- 1 whole freshwater fish, such as trout, about 400 g/14 oz, gutted
- 1 heaped tbsp plain flour
- pinch of salt
- 125 ml/4 fl oz water
- vegetable or groundnut oil, for deep-frying
- shredded spring onion, to garnish

chilli bean sauce

- 125 ml/4 fl oz vegetable or groundnut oil
- 1 tsp dried chilli flakes
- 1 garlic clove, finely chopped
- 1 tsp finely chopped fresh ginger
- 1 tbsp chilli bean sauce
- ½ tsp white pepper
- 2 tsp sugar
- 1 tbsp white rice vinegar
- 1 tsp finely chopped spring onion

1 Rinse the fish inside and out under cold running water and pat dry with kitchen paper. Mix together the flour, salt and water to create a light batter. Coat the fish with the batter.

2 Heat enough oil for deep-frying in a wok, deep-fat fryer or heavy-based pan to 180–190°C/350–375°F, or until a cube of bread browns in 30 seconds. Deep-fry the fish on one side at a time until the skin is crisp and golden brown. Drain, then transfer to a serving platter and keep warm.

3 To make the sauce, first heat all but 1 tablespoon of the oil in a small saucepan and, when smoking, pour over the dried chilli flakes. Set aside.

4 In a preheated wok or deep saucepan, heat the remaining oil and stir-fry the garlic and ginger until fragrant. Stir in the chilli bean sauce, then add the oil and chilli flake mixture. Season with the pepper, sugar and vinegar. Turn off the heat and stir in the chopped spring onion. Tip the sauce over the fish, garnish with shredded spring onion and serve immediately.

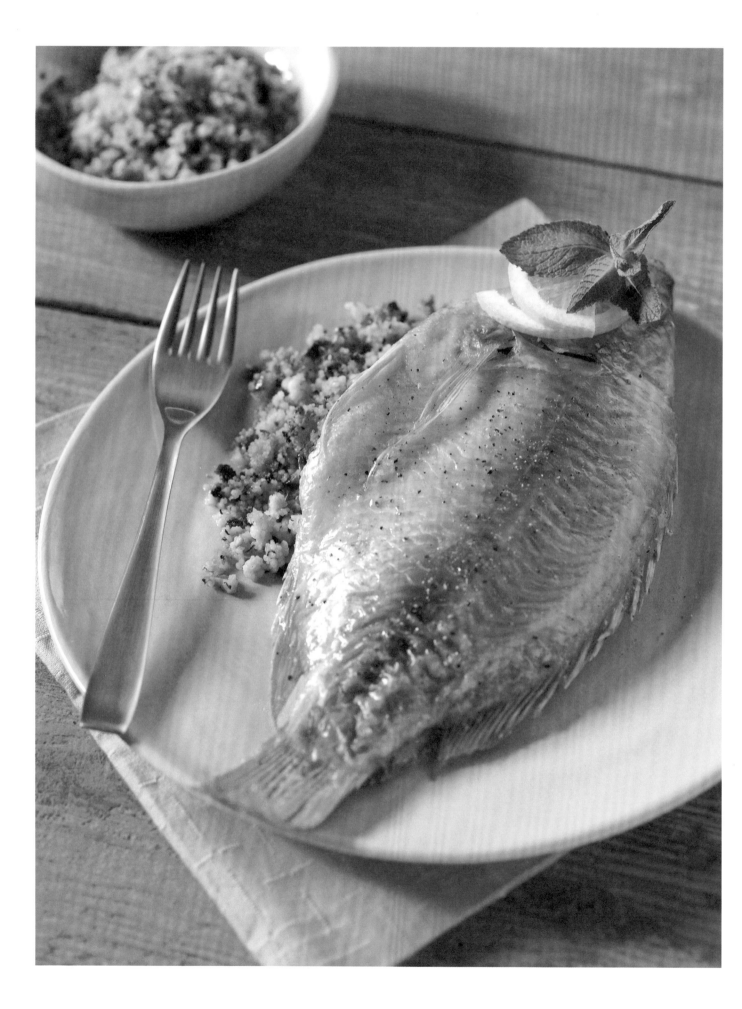

Tilapia with Mint Couscous

Serves 4

ingredients

- 4 whole tilapia, each about 350 g/12 oz, scaled, gutted and boned
- 4 tbsp olive oil
- 1 red onion, finely chopped
- 1 garlic clove, finely chopped
- 300 ml/10 fl oz fish stock (see page 20)
- 115 g/4 oz couscous
- 2 tbsp chopped fresh mint, plus extra sprigs to garnish
- butter, for greasing
- 55 g/2 oz pistachio nuts, finely chopped
- 2 tbsp lemon juice
- salt and pepper
- lemon slices, to garnish

1 Rinse the fish inside and out under cold running water and pat dry with kitchen paper.

2 Heat half the oil in a saucepan. Add the onion and cook over a low heat, stirring occasionally, for 5 minutes, until softened. Add the garlic and cook, stirring, for a further 2 minutes. Pour in the stock and stir in the couscous and chopped mint. Bring to the boil, then remove the pan from the heat and set aside for 15 minutes, until all the liquid has been absorbed.

3 Meanwhile, preheat the oven to 200°C/400°F/Gas Mark 6. Grease an ovenproof dish, large enough to hold all the fish, with butter.

4 Season the fish inside and out with salt and pepper. Fluff up the couscous mixture with a fork and stir in the nuts, then divide it among the cavities of the fish. Place the fish in the prepared dish and drizzle with the remaining oil.

5 Bake in the preheated oven for 20 minutes, until the flesh flakes easily. Transfer the fish to warmed serving plates and sprinkle with the lemon juice. Garnish with mint sprigs and lemon slices, and serve immediately.

Tilapia with Watercress Sauce

Serves 4

ingredients

- 4 tilapia fillets, each about 175 g/6 oz, skinned
- juice of ½ lemon
- 5 tbsp olive oil
- 1 shallot, finely chopped
- 1 garlic clove, finely chopped
- 115 g/4 oz watercress, finely chopped
- 250 ml/9 fl oz crème fraîche
- salt and pepper
- watercress sprigs, to garnish
- cooked new potatoes, to serve

1 Rinse the fish under cold running water and pat dry with kitchen paper. Sprinkle the fish fillets with the lemon juice and season to taste with salt and pepper. Heat 3 tablespoons of the oil in a frying pan. Add the fish and cook over a medium–low heat for 3–4 minutes on each side.

2 Meanwhile, heat the remaining oil in a saucepan. Add the shallot and garlic and cook over a low heat, stirring occasionally, for 5 minutes, until soft. Stir in the watercress and cook, stirring occasionally, for 2 minutes, until wilted. Stir in the crème fraîche, season to taste with salt and pepper, and heat gently.

3 Using a fish slice, transfer the fish fillets to warmed serving plates. Spoon the sauce over them, garnish with watercress sprigs and serve immediately with new potatoes.

Fennel-roasted
Whole Tilapia

Serves 4

ingredients

- 1 large whole tilapia, about 2 kg/4 lb 8 oz, gutted but on the bone
- 4 garlic cloves, roughly chopped
- 4 bay leaves
- 3 fresh thyme sprigs
- handful of fresh parsley
- 2 lemons, sliced
- 1 large fennel bulb, sliced and fronds reserved
- 55 g/2 oz butter, thinly sliced, plus extra for greasing
- 100 ml/3½ fl oz white wine
- salt and pepper

1 Preheat the oven to 190°C/375°F/ Gas Mark 5. Rinse the fish inside and out under cold running water and pat dry with kitchen paper. Season to taste with salt and pepper and put 2 of the garlic cloves, 2 of the bay leaves, a third of the herbs and 6 of the lemon slices inside the cavity.

2 Lay two large sheets of foil on top of each other (they should be wide enough to double-wrap the whole fish), and grease with butter to prevent the fish from sticking. Pull the sides up a little so the ingredients don't spill.

3 Place half of the remaining herbs and lemon slices on the foil with half of the fennel and butter and lay the fish on top. Scatter the remaining herbs, lemon, fennel and butter on top, pour over the wine and season to taste with salt and pepper.

4 Wrap the fish loosely, folding over the ends of the foil. Put the package in a roasting tin and bake in the preheated oven for 30–40 minutes, until the flesh flakes easily.

5 Open the package at the table (watch out for the steam). Allow everyone to serve themselves from one side, then turn the fish over and repeat.

Catfish Stew

Serves 4

ingredients
- 2 tsp garlic granules
- 1 tsp celery salt
- 1 tsp pepper
- 1 tsp curry powder
- 1 tsp paprika
- pinch of caster sugar
- 4–8 slices catfish or rockfish, about 900 g/2 lb total weight
- 2 tbsp red wine vinegar
- 40 g/1½ oz plain flour
- 6 tbsp sunflower oil
- 1 onion, finely chopped
- 2 garlic cloves, finely chopped
- 280 g/10 oz tomatoes, peeled and chopped
- 1 fresh marjoram sprig
- 600 ml/1 pint fish stock (see page 20)
- ¼ tsp ground cumin
- ¼ tsp ground cinnamon
- 2 fresh red or green chillies, deseeded and finely chopped
- 1 red pepper, deseeded and finely chopped
- 1 yellow pepper, deseeded and finely chopped
- salt
- fresh coriander sprigs, to garnish
- fresh crusty bread, to serve

1 Mix together the garlic granules, celery salt, pepper, curry powder, paprika and sugar in a small bowl.

2 Rinse the fish under cold running water and pat dry with kitchen paper. Place the fish in a non-metallic dish and sprinkle with half the spice mixture. Turn the fish over and sprinkle with the remaining spice mixture. Add the vinegar and turn to coat. Cover with clingfilm and set aside in a cool place to marinate for 1 hour.

3 Spread out the flour in a shallow dish. Drain the fish and dip the slices in the flour to coat, shaking off any excess.

4 Heat 4 tablespoons of the oil in a frying pan. Add the fish and cook over a medium heat for 2–3 minutes on each side. Remove with a fish slice and set aside.

5 Wipe out the frying pan with kitchen paper, add the remaining oil and heat. Add the onion and cook over a low heat, stirring occasionally, for 5 minutes, until soft. Add the chopped garlic and cook, stirring, for a further 2 minutes. Add the tomatoes and marjoram, increase the heat to medium and cook, stirring occasionally, for 8 minutes.

6 Stir in the stock, cumin and cinnamon and add the fish, chillies and peppers. Bring to the boil, then reduce the heat and simmer for 8–10 minutes, until the fish flakes easily and the sauce has thickened. Season to taste with salt, garnish with coriander sprigs and serve immediately with crusty bread.

Baked Catfish

Serves 4

ingredients

- butter, for greasing
- 4 catfish or rockfish fillets, each about 175 g/6 oz, skinned
- 115 g/4 oz unsalted peanuts, finely ground
- 4 tbsp soured cream
- 2 tbsp milk
- 4 tbsp wholegrain mustard
- 4 spring onions, finely chopped
- salad leaves and lime wedges, to garnish

1 Preheat the oven to 230°C/450°F/ Gas Mark 8. Generously grease a baking tray with butter. Rinse the fish under cold running water and pat dry with kitchen paper. Spread out the ground peanuts in a shallow dish.

2 Mix together the soured cream, milk, mustard and spring onions in a bowl. Dip the fish fillets in the mixture to coat. You may need to do this more than once to ensure that they are completely covered. Gently roll the fish fillets in the ground peanuts to coat.

3 Place the fish on the prepared baking tray and bake in the preheated oven for 8–10 minutes, until the flesh flakes easily. Serve immediately, garnished with salad leaves and lime wedges.

Fried Catfish Fillets

Serves 4

ingredients
- 70 g/2½ oz plain flour
- 2 eggs
- 225 g/8 oz polenta
- ½ tsp dried thyme
- pinch of cayenne pepper
- 900 g/2 lb catfish fillets, skinned
- sunflower oil, for shallow-frying
- salt and pepper

to serve
- salad leaves
- lemon wedges
- mayonnaise (see page 22)

1 Put the flour on a plate. Beat the eggs in a shallow bowl. Put the polenta on a separate plate and season with the thyme, cayenne pepper, and salt and pepper to taste.

2 Rinse the fish under cold running water and pat dry with kitchen paper. Dust the catfish fillets with the flour on both sides, shaking off any excess, dip into the beaten eggs, then pat the polenta onto both sides.

3 Heat about 5 cm/2 inches of oil in a large frying pan over a medium heat. Add as many catfish fillets as will fit without overcrowding the frying pan and cook for 2 minutes, or until the coating is golden brown.

4 Turn the catfish fillets over and cook for a further 2 minutes, or until the flesh flakes easily. Remove from the frying pan with a slotted spoon and drain on kitchen paper. Keep warm while cooking the remaining fillets, if necessary. Add more oil to the frying pan as needed.

5 Serve the fried catfish with salad leaves and lemon wedges, accompanied by some mayonnaise.

Chapter 2
Round Seafish

The Round Seafish Directory

The following is a guide to all the main species of round seafish that can be eaten, listed by their common names, although some fish, confusingly, are known by a variety of different names. The potted profile for each fish details the various forms in which it can be purchased, for example whole or in fillets, fresh or canned, and the most suitable cooking methods.

Coley

Hoki

Sea Bass

Cod

Sea Bass/Bass

This large, sleek fish, similar in shape to the salmon, has dark, silver-grey scales, which should be removed before cooking, and a white belly. Its firm, white flesh has an excellent flavour. It can be bought whole or in cutlets or fillets and is suitable for poaching or steaming.

Cod

This very popular, white-fleshed fish varies enormously in size and is available whole, which is particularly suitable for baking, poaching or steaming, and in fillets and cutlets, which can be fried or grilled. It is commonly used in cooked dishes such as fish pie. Much of it is frozen aboard fishing boats. It is also available salted, smoked and dried. Cod's roe is available fresh and smoked.

Coley/Saithe/Coalfish

Coley is related to the cod family and has pinkish-grey flesh that becomes white when cooked. Usually available as fillets or cutlets, it can be used in the same way as cod but, as it can be dry, is not suitable for grilling. It is used in soups, stews and fish pies.

Hoki

Imported from New Zealand, hoki is related to hake, which, in turn, is a member of the cod family. Its white flesh is firm, contains very few bones and has a mild flavour. It is sold in fillets or pieces and can be baked, fried or grilled.

Haddock

This fish has a firm, white flesh and is closely related to cod, although it is usually smaller and can be distinguished by the dark streak that runs down its back and the two black marks either side of its gills. Sold as fillets or cutlets, it is interchangeable with cod in recipes and is used as an alternative when serving fish and chips. Haddock is often smoked – it is used as such in the well-known dish kedgeree.

Monkfish/Angler Fish

This deep sea fish has such a large, ugly head that usually only the tail is sold, boned as a whole piece or skinned and filleted. The monkfish is a species that matures late and is therefore vulnerable to overfishing.

Many species are vulnerable to overfishing – see the best choices to
make in the MCS Good Fish Guide at www.mcsuk.org

Monkfish

Haddock

Salmon

Sea Trout

Parrot Fish

This beautiful tropical fish, with skin ranging in colour from turquoise and green to pink and violet, and its round, beak-like face really does look like a parrot. Its flesh is white and firm and it is best cooked whole.

Pomfret

This silver, fairly small fish from warm waters is a round fish but, like the John Dory, is laterally compressed and therefore prepared as though a flat fish. It is similar to butterfish, which is popular in America. The flesh is white and delicate, and it can be stuffed and baked whole or filleted and fried or grilled.

Red Mullet

Red mullet, of which there are several species, is unrelated to grey mullet. It looks attractive, with its crimson skin. It has a firm, white flesh, which has a delicate flavour. Its liver, too, is considered a delicacy, which is why it is usually sold uncleaned. For this reason, it should be eaten fresh before it deteriorates. It must be scaled before cooking and is usually cooked whole, fried, grilled or baked.

Salmon

Most salmon varieties mature at sea and then return to coastal rivers and streams to spawn. Atlantic salmon (wild salmon) and farmed salmon are available, and increased harvests of farmed salmon have made this popular fish more affordable. Salmon has a high fat content and a firm flesh, which can be pink to dark red. It can be poached or baked whole and its cutlets or fillets can be fried or grilled. Its red roe is available as salmon caviar, although this description really applies only to sturgeon roe. It is also popular canned and smoked. Smoked salmon is dry-salted before being smoked and is sold in fillets, which are cut into paper-thin slices.

Salmon Trout/Sea Trout

This fish is often confused with salmon as it also returns from the sea to spawn in coastal rivers. It is smaller than salmon, but larger than trout, has pale pink flesh and can be used in the same way as salmon or trout. However, it is too delicate for smoking. It can be purchased whole or as fillets.

Grey Mullet

Whiting

Barracuda

Whiting

This fish, related to hake, is fairly small and has pale brown skin and a cream belly. Its flesh is white and very soft, with a bland flavour. It can be bought fresh, either whole or in fillets, as well as smoked or salted. It is suitable for frying, grilling, poaching or steaming.

Sea Bream

There are numerous varieties of this large fish, including the red, black, white, pink, ray and gilt-head sea bream. All have firm, white flesh, but the red bream is generally considered to have the best flavour. It is usually cooked whole and can be stuffed and baked, grilled or braised. Its interesting story is that they start life as males and later turn into females!

Grey Mullet

This fish, unrelated to the red mullet, looks and tastes similar to sea bass. It has firm, white flesh and can be bought whole or in fillets and is best baked or grilled.

Barracuda

This large, fierce fish from warm waters has white flesh with a firm texture. Small barracuda can be filleted and are suitable for baking, frying, grilling, poaching, steaming and for using in soups and stews. Never eat barracuda raw, nor eat its liver, as it can be toxic.

Hake

This large fish is a member of the cod family, but has a slightly firmer, white flesh. Large hake are cut into fillets or cutlets and these are usually poached, but they can also be fried or grilled. Small hake are sold whole. Smoked hake is also available, as well as salted hake, which is prepared and used in the same way as salt cod.

Sea Bream

Mackerel

Herring

John Dory

Herring

This is a small, very oily fish, available whole or filleted, that can be fried or grilled or stuffed and baked. Due to its oiliness, the herring is ideal for preserving. Rollmop herrings are raw herrings, boned, rolled up with chopped onions, gherkins and peppercorns and then marinated in spiced vinegar. Herrings are also smoked. Kippers are the most popular form and are sold in fillets or whole, often in pairs. Ideally, dye should not be used in the process. Buckling is another version of smoked herring, one that is often considered the best, and lightly salted bloaters and smoked herrings are also available. Herrings can be preserved between layers of salt. Canned herring is also popular.

John Dory/Dory

In most parts of the world, John Dory is called St Peter or St Pierre (not to be confused with St Peter's Fish), but not in the UK, Greece or Portugal. Although strictly speaking a round fish, John Dory is laterally compressed and therefore prepared as a flat fish, from which there is little flesh and much waste. It has an ugly head with a very large jaw and a large mark on its side like a thumb print. When fresh it

is golden in colour and its firm, white flesh has a delicate flavour. It is usually filleted and fried and it is also a traditional ingredient in the Mediterranean fish stew bouillabaisse.

Mackerel

This fish, with its striking black markings and silver belly, is particularly oily, which makes it ideal for frying and grilling or stuffing and baking.

As its dark flesh has a distinctive flavour, it is often accompanied by a sharp-flavoured sauce, such as gooseberry. Mackerel is available whole or in fillets, as well as canned or smoked. Smoked mackerel has a rich, strong flavour and is sold in fillets that are sometimes peppered or herbed to enhance the flavour of the fish.

Dolphin Fish/Mahi-Mahi/Dorado

Found in warm waters, this is a stunningly attractive fish with a streamlined silver body, and black and gold spots that fade once it is caught. Small fish are sold whole, whereas larger fish are sold in cutlets and fillets. Its flesh is firm and well flavoured, and it is very versatile as it can be fried, grilled and cooked in a pie.

Red Snapper

Sardine

Swordfish

Pollack

Pollack is closely related to cod, although it is usually smaller and its flavour is not as good. Most is frozen aboard fishing boats. It is cooked in the same way as cod and is ideal in mixed fish soups.

Red Snapper

This large fish, identified by its vivid rose-pink skin and red eyes, has white, creamy flesh and is cut into fillets or cutlets, which can be fried, grilled, poached or steamed. Small ones can be stuffed and baked whole.

Sardine/Pilchard

These oily, strong-flavoured fish vary in size. The smaller fish are called sardines, whereas the larger, mature fish are known as pilchards, three or four of which make one serving. Sold fresh, they can be fried, grilled or baked. Canned sardines can be eaten whole as the preserving process softens their bones.

Swordfish

Swordfish is an enormous fish and is sold as cutlets or chunks. Its firm, dense texture makes it perfect for grilling and frying, although it can also be poached, steamed or baked.

Conger Eel/Moray Eel

These are snake-like fish whose bodies can grow up to 2.5 metres/8 feet. The conger eel was once part of the staple diet of the Cornish people, as it was easily caught along the rocky coastline of southern England. It is also available smoked. The moray eel, of which there are several species, is a cousin of the conger eel, but is much smaller. Both conger and moray eels have firm, white flesh and are usually sold in cutlets. They can be roasted or baked and are good in pies, soups and stews.

Tuna

Anchovy

Pompano

Tuna

There are many species of this large fish, with its dark blue back and silver-grey sides and belly, including skipjack, yellowfin, bluefin, albacore and big-eye. Its flesh varies in colour from pale pink to dark red and it has a firm, dense texture. It can be bought in chunks or steaks, for frying, grilling, braising or poaching, but it should not be overcooked as it tends to dry out during cooking. Tuna is also sold canned in oil, brine or spring water.

Pompano

This warmwater fish has a silver skin and fatty flesh. It can be bought whole or in fillets. Its skin should be removed before cooking. It can be baked, fried, grilled, steamed, poached or used in soups and stews.

Anchovy

These small fish are identified by their large mouths, which almost stretch back to their gills. They are high in fat and, although occasionally available fresh, most are filleted, cured in salt and oil and then canned. They are sold flat or rolled.

Trimming & Scaling a Round Seafish

Before preparing fish it must be cleaned. This means removing the entrails and gills and sometimes the scales and fins. Your fish supplier with often do this for you, otherwise the following guidelines provide a step-by-step method.

Trimming a round seafish

If desired, using kitchen scissors, cut off the gills and fins if the fish is to be served whole. The head and tail may also be cut off using a sharp knife. Rinse the cavity under cold running water. Fins and scales don't need to be removed if the fish is to be filleted or the skin is to be removed after cooking, or in the case of trout, where the scales are part of the skin.

Scaling a round seafish

This is necessary for fish such as sea bass, salmon and snapper. Using the back of a knife or a fish scaler, scrape from the tail to the head, away from the direction of the scales, in short, firm strokes. As scales have a tendency to fly everywhere, you might find this easier if you put the fish in the sink, either in a large polythene bag or covered with a large tea towel. Rinse under cold running water and dry on kitchen paper.

Opposite: **Grilled Red Snapper with Garlic (see page 98)**

Gutting & Pocket-gutting
Round Seafish

Although your fish supplier should do this for you, it's a useful technique to learn, as you may be lucky enough to buy your fish straight from the boat or even catch your own!

> Gutting round seafish

1 To remove the entrails, make a slit along the belly from the gills to the tail vent. Pull out the insides and clean away any blood in the cavity.

2 Remove the kidneys by running your thumbnail along the underside of the spine.

3 Rub with a little coarse sea salt to remove the black skin. Rinse under cold water and dry with kitchen paper.

> Pocket-gutting round seafish

This is suitable for creating a pocket in a fish while keeping the body intact. The fish is gutted through the gills, but it is not as simple a method as gutting a round seafish along its belly.

1 Using a sharp knife, cut the end of the gut away from the anus, then open the gill covering and make a slit to reveal the throat.

2 With your fingers, pull out the guts through the throat cavity. Rinse under cold water, removing any remaining innards, and dry on kitchen paper.

Filleting Large & Small
Round Seafish

Very large round fish, such as John Dory, can be filleted into four, following the flat fish method, or the whole sides can be lifted as described here and then each cut into two fillets. Butterfly boning is a suitable filleting method for small fish such as herrings and sardines that are usually cooked whole.

> Filleting large round seafish

1 Put the fish on its side on a chopping board. Make an angular cut around the gills to the top of the head. It is not necessary to remove either the head or the tail.

2 Cut along the backbone from the head to the tail in order to expose the backbone.

3 With smooth cutting strokes, working from head to tail, separate the flesh from the bones. Turn the flesh over and repeat on the other side, but this time working from tail to head.

> Filleting small round seafish

1 Cut off the head and fins. Make a slit along the belly from the gills to the tail vent and remove the guts. Rinse under cold running water. Put the fish, skin-side up, on a chopping board and, with the heel of your hand, press firmly down on the backbone to loosen it.

2 Turn the fish over, cut the backbone near the head, then ease the backbone out with your fingers. Remove any pinbones, as described in Pinboning fish (see page 67), then cut off the tail.

Skinning & Pinboning Whole
Round Seafish & Fish Fillets

Whole round seafish are usually cooked with the skin on, which is then removed before serving. The cooking process makes the skin easier to remove, but you must take great care not to damage the soft cooked flesh while removing the skin. Fish fillets are often skinned raw.

> Skinning whole round seafish

1 Should you wish to remove the skin before cooking, using a sharp knife, cut along the backbone and across the skin just below the head.

2 With salted fingers, gently pull the skin down towards the tail, being careful not to break the flesh. Turn the fish over and repeat on the other side.

> Skinning fish fillets

> Pinboning fish

Put the fish fillet, skin-side down, on a chopping board. Gripping the fillet firmly in one hand with a cloth or kitchen paper and with a knife held at an angle, remove the flesh by making a gentle sawing action away from you. A large pinch of salt may help you to grip the fish.

Small pinbones are to be found at the top of the flesh of round fish fillets. To remove them, feel for the bones with your fingertips and then remove them using a pair of tweezers.

Roasted Salmon with
Lemon & Herbs

Serves 4

ingredients
- 6 tbsp extra virgin olive oil
- 1 onion, sliced
- 1 leek, trimmed and sliced
- juice of ½ lemon
- 2 tbsp chopped fresh parsley
- 2 tbsp chopped fresh dill
- 500 g/1 lb 2 oz salmon fillets
- salt and pepper
- freshly cooked baby spinach leaves and lemon wedges, to serve

1 Preheat the oven to 200°C/400°F/ Gas Mark 6. Heat 1 tablespoon of the oil in a frying pan over a medium heat. Add the onion and leek and cook, stirring, for about 4 minutes, until slightly soft.

2 Meanwhile, put the remaining oil in a small bowl with the lemon juice, herbs, and salt and pepper to taste. Stir together well. Rinse the fish under cold running water, then pat dry with kitchen paper. Arrange the fish in an ovenproof baking dish.

3 Remove the frying pan from the heat and spread the onion and leek over the fish. Pour the oil mixture over the top, ensuring that everything is well coated. Bake in the preheated oven for about 10 minutes, or until the fish is cooked through.

4 Arrange the cooked spinach on warmed serving plates. Remove the fish and vegetables from the oven and arrange on top of the spinach. Serve immediately, accompanied by the lemon wedges.

Teriyaki Salmon Fillets
with Chinese Noodles

Serves 4

ingredients

- 4 salmon fillets, each about 200 g/7 oz
- 125 ml/4 fl oz teriyaki marinade
- 1 shallot, sliced
- 2-cm/¾-inch piece fresh ginger, finely chopped
- 2 carrots, sliced
- 115 g/4 oz closed-cup mushrooms, sliced
- 1.2 litres/2 pints vegetable stock
- 250 g/9 oz dried medium egg noodles
- 115 g/4 oz frozen peas
- 175 g/6 oz Chinese leaves, shredded
- 4 spring onions, sliced

1 Rinse the fish under cold running water and pat dry with kitchen paper. Arrange the salmon fillets, skin-side up, in a dish just large enough to fit them in a single layer.

2 Mix the teriyaki marinade with the shallot and ginger in a small bowl and pour over the salmon. Cover and leave to marinate in the refrigerator for at least 1 hour, turning the salmon over halfway through the marinating time.

3 Put the carrots, mushrooms and stock into a large saucepan. Drain the salmon, reserving the marinade, and place, skin-side down, on a baking tray. Pour the reserved marinade into the saucepan and bring to the boil. Reduce the heat, cover and simmer for 10 minutes.

4 Meanwhile, preheat the grill. Cook the salmon under the preheated grill for 10–15 minutes, depending on the thickness of the fillets, until the flesh turns pink and flakes easily. Remove from under the grill and keep warm.

5 Add the noodles and peas to the saucepan and return to the boil. Reduce the heat, cover and simmer for 5 minutes, or until the noodles are tender. Stir in the Chinese leaves and spring onions and heat through for 1 minute.

6 Carefully drain off 300 ml/10 fl oz of the cooking liquid into a small heatproof jug and reserve. Drain and discard the remaining cooking liquid. Divide the noodles and vegetables among warmed serving bowls and top each with a salmon fillet. Pour over the reserved cooking liquid and serve immediately.

Salmon with Warm Lemon & Olive Dressing

Serves 4

ingredients
- 4 salmon fillets, each about 175 g/6 oz
- 2 tbsp olive oil
- juice of ½ lemon
- salt
- cooked new potatoes, to serve

dressing
- handful of fresh basil leaves
- 2 tbsp snipped fresh chives
- 1 garlic clove, crushed
- 1 tsp wholegrain mustard
- ½ tsp caster sugar
- juice of ½ lemon
- 200 ml/7 fl oz extra virgin olive oil
- finely chopped rind of ½ preserved lemon
- 10 stoned black olives, finely chopped

1 Preheat the oven to 200°C/400°F/ Gas Mark 6. Rinse the salmon under cold running water and pat dry with kitchen paper.

2 To make the dressing, put the herbs, garlic, mustard, sugar, lemon juice and extra virgin olive oil in a blender or food processor and process until smooth. Pour the mixture into a small saucepan, add the preserved lemon rind and olives, and warm over a gentle heat.

3 Meanwhile, heat the olive oil in a frying pan over a medium heat, add the salmon fillets, skin-side down, and cook for 3 minutes, or until the skin is golden and crisp. Lay the fish in a roasting tin, skin-side up, squeeze over the lemon juice and season with a little salt.

4 Roast in the preheated oven for 5 minutes, or until the fish is just cooked through – the exact timing will depend on the thickness of the fillets. Transfer to warmed serving plates and spoon over the dressing. Serve immediately with new potatoes.

Tuna with a Chilli Crust

Serves 4

ingredients
- 1 small bunch of fresh coriander or flat-leaf parsley
- 3–4 dried red chillies, crushed
- 2 tbsp sesame seeds
- 1 egg white
- 4 tuna steaks, each about 140–175 g/5–6 oz
- 2–3 tbsp sunflower oil
- salt and pepper
- lime wedges, to garnish

1 Chop the coriander, leaving a few leaves whole to garnish. Mix the crushed chillies, chopped coriander and sesame seeds together in a shallow dish and season to taste with salt and pepper. Lightly beat the egg white with a fork in a separate shallow dish.

2 Rinse the tuna under cold running water and pat dry with kitchen paper. Dip the tuna steaks first in the egg white, then in the chilli and herb mixture to coat. Gently pat the crust evenly over the fish with the palm of your hand, making sure that both sides of the steaks are well covered.

3 Heat the oil in a large heavy-based frying pan. Add the tuna and cook over a medium heat for 2 minutes, then turn over carefully, using a fish slice. Cook for a further 2 minutes, then transfer to warmed serving plates. Garnish with the lime wedges and the reserved coriander leaves, and serve immediately.

Warm Tuna &
Kidney Bean Salad

Serves 4

ingredients
- 4 tuna steaks, each about 175 g/6 oz
- 1 tbsp olive oil
- 200 g/7 oz canned kidney beans, drained and rinsed
- 100 g/3½ oz canned sweetcorn, drained
- 2 spring onions, trimmed and thinly sliced
- salt and pepper
- lime wedges, to garnish

dressing
- 5 tbsp extra virgin olive oil
- 3 tbsp balsamic vinegar
- 1 tbsp lime juice
- 1 garlic clove, chopped
- 1 tbsp chopped fresh coriander
- salt and pepper

1 Preheat a ridged griddle pan. Rinse the tuna under cold running water and pat dry with kitchen paper. Brush the tuna steaks with olive oil, then season to taste with salt and pepper.

2 Cook the tuna in the preheated griddle pan for 2 minutes, then turn over and cook on the other side for a further 2 minutes, or according to your taste, but do not overcook. Remove from the heat and allow to cool slightly.

3 To make the dressing, put all the ingredients into a small bowl and stir together well.

4 Put the kidney beans, sweetcorn and spring onions into a large bowl, pour over half of the dressing and mix together well. Divide the bean and sweetcorn salad among individual serving plates, then place a tuna steak on each one. Drizzle over the remaining dressing, garnish with lime wedges and serve immediately.

Tuna Steaks
with Catalan Sauce

Serves 4

ingredients

- 2 tbsp olive oil, plus extra for brushing
- 1 onion, chopped
- 2 red peppers, deseeded and chopped
- 1 fresh red chilli, deseeded and chopped
- 1 garlic clove, chopped
- 400 g/14 oz canned chopped tomatoes
- dash of white wine vinegar
- 50 g/1¾ oz ground almonds
- 4 tuna steaks, each about 125 g/4½ oz
- salt and pepper
- cooked French beans and lemon wedges, to serve

1 Heat the oil in a non-stick frying pan over a medium–high heat. Add the onion and peppers and cook, stirring frequently, for 10 minutes, or until soft. Add the chilli and garlic and cook, stirring, for 1 minute. Add the tomatoes and their juice, bring to a simmer and cook for 15 minutes. Stir in the vinegar.

2 Transfer the tomato mixture to a blender or food processor. Add the ground almonds and blend for 20 seconds, or until smooth. Season with a little salt and pepper to taste, and add a little water if the mixture is too thick to pour.

3 Preheat the grill to high or heat a ridged griddle pan over a high heat. Rinse the tuna under cold running water and pat dry with kitchen paper. Lightly brush with oil on both sides. Cook under the preheated grill or in the very hot griddle pan for 2 minutes on each side, or according to your taste, but do not overcook.

4 Transfer the tuna steaks to warmed plates and spoon over the sauce. Serve immediately with French beans and lemon wedges.

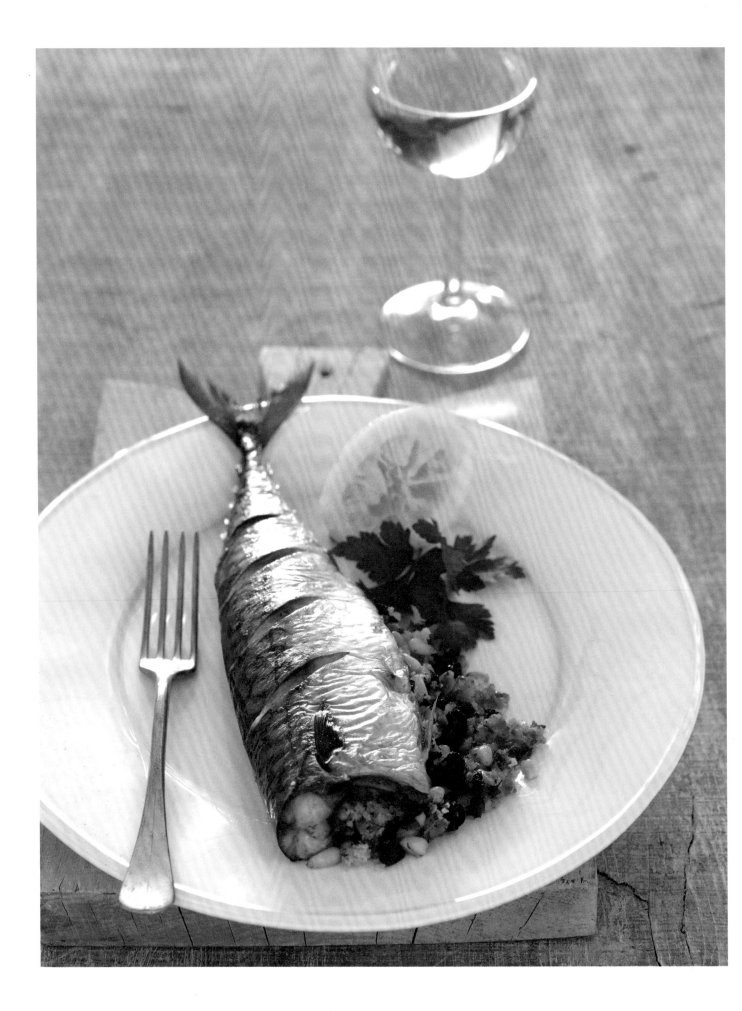

Baked Mackerel Stuffed
with Raisins & Pine Kernels

Serves 4

ingredients
- 4 whole mackerel, each about 350 g/12 oz, gutted
- 3 tbsp olive oil, plus extra for brushing
- 1 onion, finely chopped
- 100 g/3½ oz fresh breadcrumbs
- 55 g/2 oz raisins, chopped
- 100 g/3½ oz pine kernels
- grated rind and juice of 1 lemon
- 1 tbsp chopped fresh dill
- 2 tbsp chopped fresh flat-leaf parsley, plus extra sprigs to garnish
- 1 egg, beaten
- salt and pepper
- lemon wedges, to serve

1 Preheat the oven to 190°C/375°F/ Gas Mark 5. Brush an ovenproof dish, large enough to hold the fish in a single layer, with oil. Rinse the fish inside and out under cold running water and pat dry with kitchen paper.

2 Heat 2 tablespoons of the oil in a large heavy-based frying pan, add the onion and fry for 5 minutes, until soft. Remove from the heat.

3 Put the breadcrumbs, raisins, pine kernels, lemon rind, dill, parsley, and salt and pepper to taste in a large bowl. Add the onion and egg, and mix well together.

4 Press the stuffing mixture into the cavities of the fish and place in the prepared dish. Using a sharp knife, make diagonal slashes along each fish. Drizzle over the lemon juice and the remaining oil.

5 Bake the fish, uncovered, in the preheated oven for 30–45 minutes, basting twice during cooking, until tender. Serve hot, garnished with parsley sprigs and accompanied by lemon wedges.

Grilled Sardines
with Rosemary

Serves 4

ingredients
- 8 whole sardines, gutted and scaled
- olive oil, for brushing
- 16 small fresh rosemary sprigs
- salt and pepper
- lemon wedges, to serve

1 Preheat the grill to high. Rinse the fish inside and out under cold running water and pat dry with kitchen paper.

2 Brush the sardines with oil. Place two rosemary sprigs in the cavity of each fish and sprinkle a little salt on top. If you have a fish cage, put the fish into that.

3 Place under the preheated grill and cook for about 2–3 minutes on each side until the skin browns a little (be careful not to cook for longer as they can overcook and dry out). Remove from the heat and season to taste with salt and pepper.

4 Serve on warmed plates with the lemon wedges for squeezing over.

Crispy Parmesan-coated
Sea Bass

Serves 4

ingredients

- 4 sea bass fillets, each about 125 g/4½ oz, skin on and pin boned
- 3 tbsp olive oil
- juice and grated rind of 1 lemon
- 100 g/3½ oz Parmesan cheese, finely grated
- 1 small bunch of fresh parsley, finely chopped
- salt and pepper
- salad leaves and lemon wedges, to serve

1 Preheat the grill to high. Rinse the fish under cold running water and pat dry with kitchen paper. Brush the grill pan with 1 tablespoon of the oil and lay the sea bass, skin-side down, in the grill pan. Drizzle over 1 tablespoon of the remaining oil, pour over the lemon juice and season to taste with salt and pepper.

2 Mix together the lemon rind, Parmesan cheese and parsley, and scatter evenly over the fish. Drizzle over the remaining oil.

3 Cook under the preheated grill for 4 minutes, or until the fish is just cooked and golden – the exact cooking time will depend on the thickness of the fillets.

4 Serve immediately with salad leaves and lemon wedges.

Sea Bream with Fennel &
Tomato Butter Sauce

Serves 4

ingredients
- 4 sea bream fillets, each about 175 g/6 oz
- 2 tbsp olive oil
- salt and pepper
- fresh flat-leaf parsley sprigs, to garnish

baked fennel
- 4 fennel bulbs, trimmed
- 1 tbsp caster sugar
- juice of ½ lemon
- 6 tbsp olive oil
- 2–3 tbsp pastis (optional)
- salt and pepper

tomato butter sauce
- 8 large vine-ripened tomatoes
- 1 tbsp extra virgin olive oil
- 1 tbsp tomato ketchup
- 75 g/2¾ oz butter, cut into cubes
- salt and pepper

1 Preheat the oven to 200°C/400°F/ Gas Mark 6. Rinse the fish under cold running water and pat dry with kitchen paper.

2 For the baked fennel, slice the fennel bulbs lengthways and put in a casserole. Sprinkle with the sugar and lemon juice. Season to taste with salt and pepper and pour over the olive oil. Cover with foil and bake in the preheated oven for 30 minutes, or until tender. Remove from the oven, pour over the pastis, if using, and return to the oven, uncovered, for a further 10 minutes. If you are not using the pastis, simply uncover and return to the oven.

3 Meanwhile, to make the sauce, put the tomatoes in a food processor and process to a purée. Pass through a sieve into a medium saucepan. Heat gently, then stir in the extra virgin olive oil and tomato ketchup. Set aside.

4 Brush the fish fillets with a little of the olive oil and season lightly with salt and pepper. Heat the remaining oil in an ovenproof frying pan over a medium–high heat, add the fish fillets, skin-side down, and cook for 1 minute. Turn the fillets over and cook for a further minute. Transfer to the oven and cook for 2–3 minutes.

5 Just before serving, gently reheat the sauce and whisk in the butter, cube by cube, until fully incorporated. Season to taste with salt and pepper.

6 Divide the fennel among warmed serving plates and top each with a fish fillet. Spoon the sauce around and serve immediately, garnished with parsley sprigs.

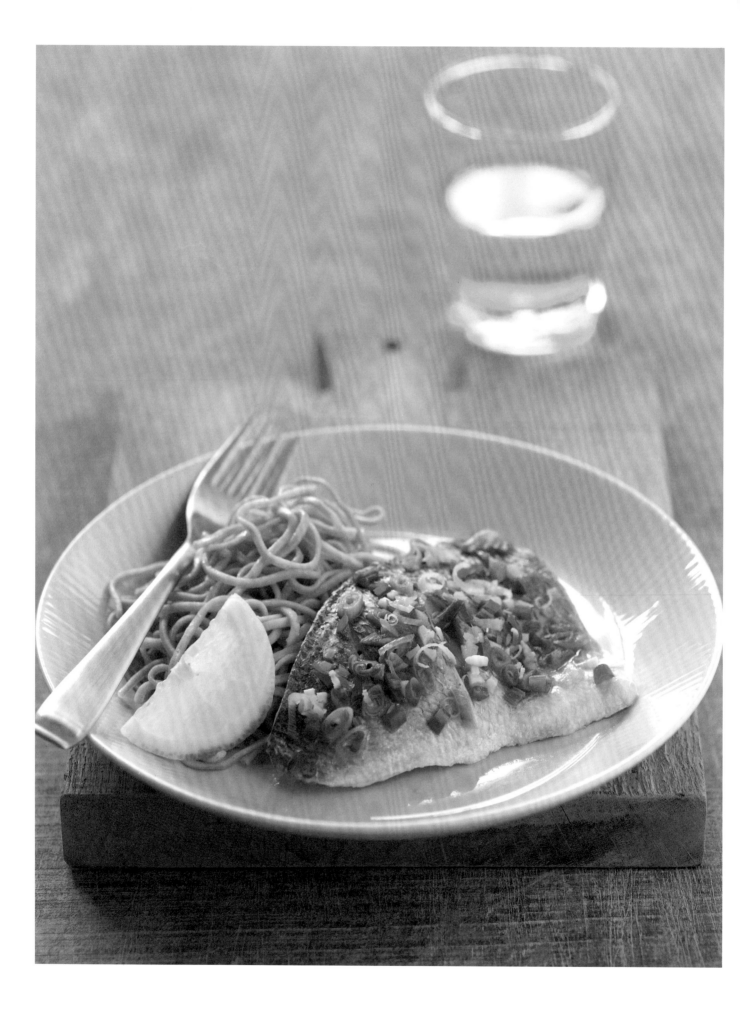

Steamed Sea Bream
with Ginger

Serves 4

ingredients
- 500 g/1 lb 2 oz sea bream or perch fillets
- 1 garlic clove, finely chopped
- 1 small fresh red chilli, deseeded and finely chopped
- 2 tbsp Thai fish sauce
- 3 tbsp lemon juice
- 100 ml/3½ fl oz fish stock (see page 20)
- 3 spring onions, trimmed and finely sliced
- 1 tbsp finely grated lemon rind
- 1 tbsp finely grated fresh ginger
- cooked egg noodles and lemon wedges, to serve

1 Rinse the fish under cold running water and pat dry with kitchen paper. Make several fairly deep diagonal cuts into the fish on both sides. Put the fish on a heatproof plate that is slightly smaller than your wok. The plate should have a rim.

2 In a separate bowl, mix together the garlic, chilli, fish sauce, lemon juice and stock. Pour this mixture over the fish. Scatter over the spring onions, lemon rind and ginger.

3 Fill a large wok with boiling water up to a depth of about 4 cm/1½ inches. Bring it back to the boil, then set a rack or trivet inside the wok. Put the plate of fish on top of the rack, then cover the wok with a lid. Reduce the heat a little and steam the fish for about 10 minutes, or until cooked through.

4 Lift out the fish and transfer to warmed serving plates. Serve with egg noodles and lemon wedges.

Roast Monkfish
with Romesco Sauce

Serves 4

ingredients

- 900 g/2 lb monkfish in 1 piece
- 2–3 slices Serrano ham
- olive oil, for brushing
- salt and pepper
- fresh flat-leaf parsley sprigs, to garnish
- sautéed potatoes and lemon wedges, to serve

romesco sauce

- 4 large ripe tomatoes
- 16 blanched almonds
- 3 large garlic cloves, unpeeled and left whole
- 1 dried sweet chilli, such as ñora, soaked for 20 minutes and patted dry
- 4 dried red chillies, soaked for 20 minutes and patted dry
- pinch of sugar
- 150 ml/5 fl oz extra virgin olive oil
- about 2 tbsp red wine vinegar
- salt and pepper

1 Preheat the oven to 180°C/350°F/ Gas Mark 4. First make the sauce. Place the tomatoes, almonds and garlic on a baking tray and roast in the preheated oven for 20 minutes, but check the almonds after about 7 minutes because they can burn quickly; remove as soon as they are golden. Peel the roasted garlic and tomatoes.

2 Put the almonds, garlic, sweet chilli and dried chillies in a food processor and process until finely chopped. Add the tomatoes and sugar and process again. With the motor running, slowly add the extra virgin olive oil through the feed tube. Add 1½ tablespoons of the vinegar and process briefly. Taste and add the remaining vinegar if needed. Season to taste with salt and pepper. Leave to stand for at least 2 hours.

3 Preheat the oven to 200°C/400°F/Gas Mark 6. Remove the thin membrane covering the monkfish, then rinse the tail under cold running water and pat dry with kitchen paper. Wrap the ham around the monkfish and brush with olive oil. Season to taste with salt and pepper. Put on a baking tray.

4 Roast the monkfish in the preheated oven for 20 minutes, until the flesh is opaque and flakes easily (test by lifting off the ham along the central bone and cut a small amount of the flesh away from the bone to see if it flakes).

5 Cut through the ham to remove the central bone and produce two thick fillets. Cut each fillet in half and transfer to individual serving plates. Stir the sauce and add a spoonful to each plate. Garnish with parsley sprigs and serve immediately with sautéed potatoes and lemon wedges.

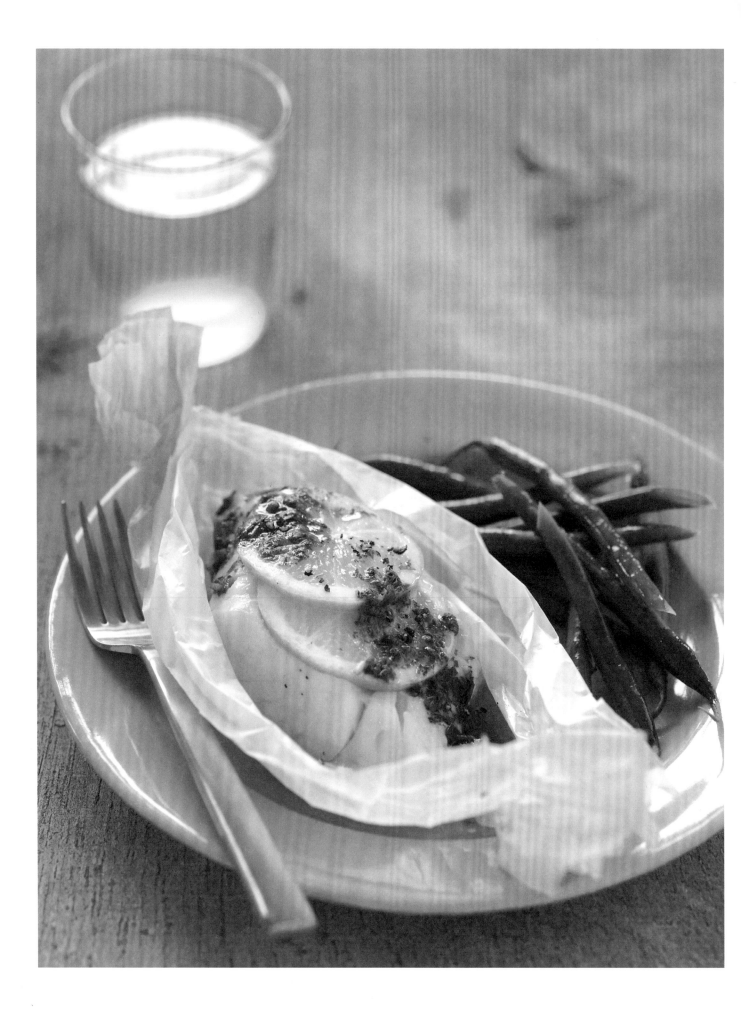

Baked Lemon Cod
with Herb Sauce

Serves 4

ingredients
- 4 thick cod fillets
- olive oil, for brushing
- 8 thin lemon slices
- salt and pepper
- cooked French beans, to serve

herb sauce
- 4 tbsp olive oil
- 1 garlic clove, crushed
- 4 tbsp chopped fresh parsley
- 2 tbsp chopped fresh mint
- juice of ½ lemon
- salt and pepper

1 Preheat the oven to 200°C/400°F/ Gas Mark 6. Rinse each cod fillet under cold running water and pat dry with kitchen paper, then brush with oil.

2 Place each fillet on a piece of baking paper large enough to enclose the fish in a parcel. Top each fillet with 2 lemon slices and season to taste with salt and pepper. Fold over the baking paper to enclose the fish and place on a baking tray. Bake in the preheated oven for 20 minutes, or until just cooked and opaque.

3 Meanwhile, to make the herb sauce, put all the ingredients into a food processor and process until smooth.

4 Carefully unfold each parcel and place on a serving plate. Pour a spoonful of herb sauce over each piece of fish before serving, accompanied by French beans.

Battered Fish with Chips

Serves 2

ingredients

- vegetable oil, for deep-frying
- 3 large potatoes
- 2 thick cod or haddock fillets, each about 175 g/6 oz
- 175 g/6 oz self-raising flour, plus extra for dusting
- 200 ml/7 fl oz cold lager
- salt and pepper
- fresh flat-leaf parsley sprigs, to garnish
- tartare sauce (see page 23) and lemon wedges, to serve

1 Heat enough oil for deep-frying in a deep-fat fryer or heavy-based saucepan to 120°C/250°F to blanch the chips. Preheat the oven to 150°C/300°F/ Gas Mark 2.

2 Peel the potatoes and cut into even-sized chips. Pat dry on kitchen paper. Fry for about 8–10 minutes, depending on size, until soft but not coloured. Remove from the oil, drain on kitchen paper and place in a warm dish in the preheated oven. Increase the temperature of the oil to 180–190°C/350–375°F, or until a cube of bread browns in 30 seconds.

3 Meanwhile, rinse the fish under cold running water and pat dry with kitchen paper. Season the fish to taste with salt and pepper and dust lightly with a little flour.

4 Sift the flour into a bowl with a little salt and whisk in most of the lager to make a thick batter. Check the consistency before adding the remaining lager; it should be very thick, like double cream.

5 Dip one of the fish fillets into the batter and allow the batter to coat it thickly. Carefully place the fish in the hot oil, then repeat with the other fillet.

6 Cook for 8–10 minutes, depending on the thickness of the fish. Turn the fillets over halfway through the cooking time. Remove the fish from the fryer, drain and keep warm.

7 Make sure the oil temperature is still at 180–190°C/350–375°F and return the chips to the fryer. Cook for a further 2–3 minutes, until golden brown and crispy. Drain and transfer to warmed serving plates with the battered fish. Garnish with parsley sprigs and serve immediately with tartare sauce and lemon wedges.

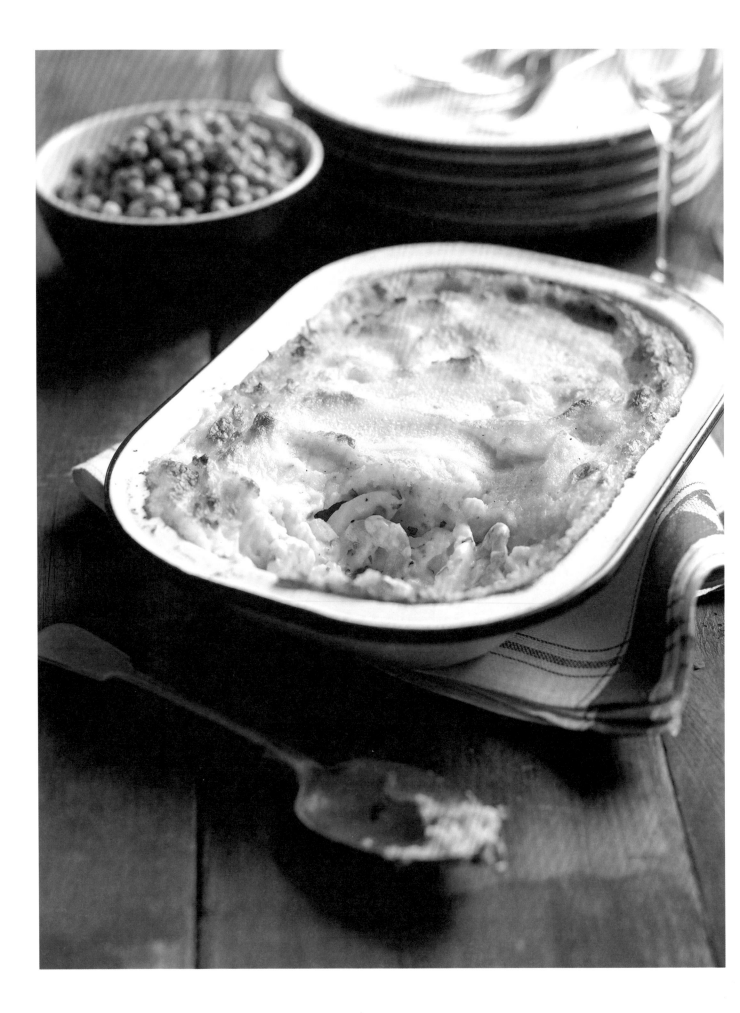

Silky Smooth Fish Pie

Serves 6-8

ingredients
- 1 kg/2 lb 4 oz floury potatoes
- 150 g/5½ oz butter, plus extra for greasing
- 500 ml/18 fl oz milk
- 600 g/1 lb 5 oz firm white fish fillets, such as cod, haddock or pollack
- 400 g/14 oz undyed smoked haddock fillet
- 3 bay leaves
- 55 g/2 oz plain flour
- handful of fresh parsley, chopped
- 250 g/9 oz cooked peeled prawns
- 4 hard-boiled eggs, shelled and quartered
- 4 tbsp melted butter
- salt and pepper
- minted peas, to serve

1 Peel and quarter the potatoes. Bring a large saucepan of lightly salted water to the boil, add the potatoes and cook for 15–20 minutes, or until tender. Drain, mash thoroughly with half of the butter and 2 tablespoons of the milk, then season to taste with salt and pepper, cover and keep warm.

2 Preheat the oven to 200°C/400°F/ Gas Mark 6. Rinse the fish under cold running water and pat dry with kitchen paper. Place the fish fillets in a shallow saucepan and pour over the remaining milk. Add the bay leaves and place over a low heat. Bring the milk to a gentle simmer and poach the fish for 4 minutes (it shouldn't be fully cooked as it will be baked later). Remove from the saucepan and place on a plate, discard the bay leaves and reserve the milk. Remove any remaining bones and skin from the fish and flake into large chunks. Put in a bowl, cover and set aside.

3 Melt the remaining butter in a saucepan, then stir in the flour to make a roux and cook, stirring occasionally, for 3 minutes. Gradually add the reserved milk, a ladleful at a time, and mix into the roux. Add the parsley, the cooked fish, the prawns and eggs. Fold carefully together. Season to taste with salt and pepper.

4 Grease a pie dish with butter and fill it with the fish mixture. Spoon the mashed potatoes on top, smoothing the surface level. Drizzle the melted butter over the whole pie, place in the preheated oven and bake for 30–40 minutes, until the top is golden brown. Serve immediately with minted peas.

Grilled Red Snapper with Garlic

Serves 4

ingredients

- 4 whole red snapper or mullet, scaled and gutted
- 2 tbsp lemon juice
- 4 tbsp olive oil, plus extra for oiling
- 2 tbsp chopped fresh herbs, such as oregano, marjoram, flat-leaf parsley or thyme
- 2 garlic cloves, finely chopped
- 2 tbsp chopped fresh flat-leaf parsley
- salt and pepper
- lemon wedges and salad leaves, to serve

1 Preheat the grill to medium. Oil the grill pan. Rinse the fish inside and out under cold running water and pat dry with kitchen paper.

2 Put the lemon juice, oil, and salt and pepper to taste in a bowl and whisk together. Brush the mixture inside and outside the fish and sprinkle over the herbs. Place on the prepared grill pan.

3 Cook the fish under the preheated grill, basting frequently, for 5 minutes on each side, until golden brown.

4 Meanwhile, mix together the garlic and parsley. Sprinkle the garlic mixture over the cooked fish and serve hot or cold, accompanied by lemon wedges and salad leaves.

Red Mullet Cooked in a Parcel

Serves 4

ingredients

- 4 whole red mullet, each about 280 g/10 oz, scaled and gutted
- 4 garlic cloves, thinly sliced lengthways
- 4 tbsp extra virgin olive oil, plus extra for brushing
- 4 tomatoes, peeled, deseeded and diced
- 2 tsp finely chopped fresh rosemary
- salt and pepper
- fresh flat-leaf parsley sprigs and thinly sliced red onions, to garnish
- fresh crusty bread, to serve

1 Preheat the oven to 200°C/400°F/ Gas Mark 6. Cut out 4 squares of greaseproof paper, each large enough to enclose a fish, and brush with a little oil.

2 Rinse the fish inside and out under cold running water, pat dry with kitchen paper and season to taste with salt and pepper. Using a sharp knife, cut 3 diagonal slits in both sides of each fish. Insert the garlic slices into the slits.

3 Combine the oil, tomatoes and rosemary in a bowl. Spoon a little of the mixture onto each of the greaseproof paper squares, then place the fish on top. Divide the remaining tomato mixture among the fish.

4 Fold up the paper around the fish, twisting it into tiny pleats to seal securely. Place the parcels on a baking tray and bake in the preheated oven for 15 minutes.

5 Transfer the parcels to warmed plates and carefully unfold. Garnish with parsley sprigs and red onion slices, and serve with crusty bread.

Spicy John Dory

Serves 4

ingredients
- 4 John Dory fillets
- 2 garlic cloves, chopped
- 2 shallots, grated
- 1 small fresh red chilli, deseeded and chopped
- 1 tbsp lemon juice

to serve
- salad leaves
- aïoli (see page 22)
- grilled tomato halves

1 Preheat the grill. Rinse the fish under cold running water and pat dry with kitchen paper.

2 Mix the garlic, shallots, chilli and lemon juice together in a separate bowl. Rub the mixture onto both sides of the fillets.

3 Cook the fish under the preheated grill for 5–8 minutes on each side, or until cooked through. Transfer the fish to warmed plates and serve immediately, accompanied by salad leaves, aïoli and grilled tomatoes.

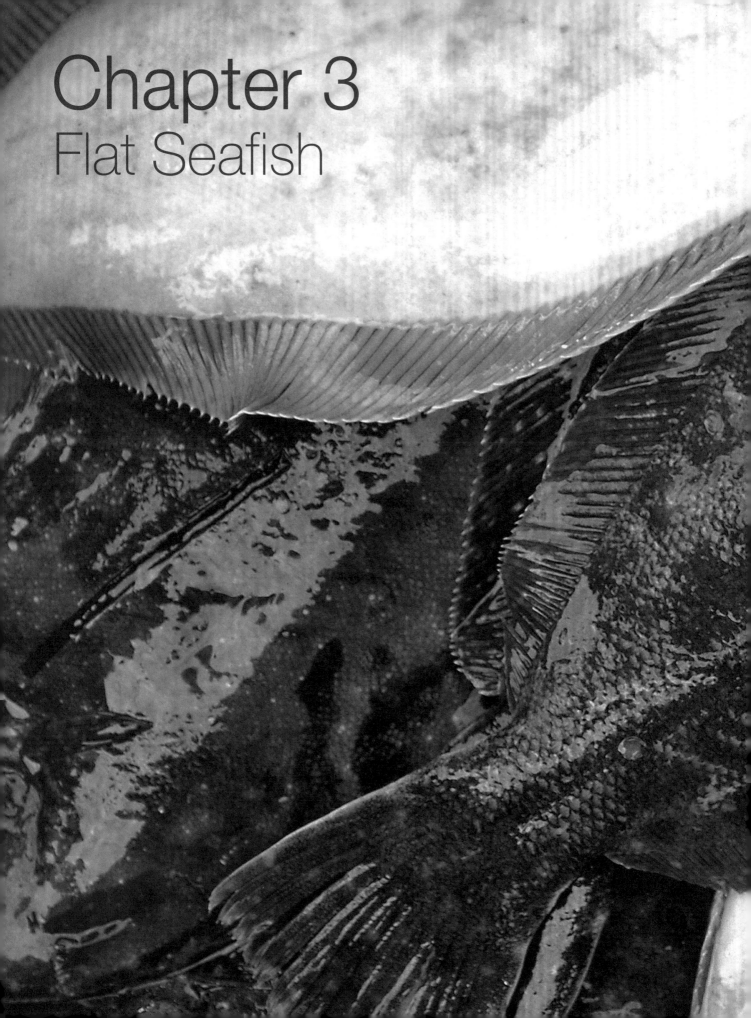

Chapter 3
Flat Seafish

The Flat Seafish Directory

The following is a guide to all the main species of flat fish that can be eaten, listed by their common names, although some fish, confusingly, are known by a variety of different names. The potted profile for each fish details the various forms in which it can be purchased, for example whole or in fillets, fresh or canned, and the most suitable cooking methods.

Flounder

Dover Sole

Turbot

Plaice

One of the most popular flat fish, it is distinguished by the large red or orange spots on its brown back. It is available whole or in fillets and its white flesh can be fried, grilled, poached, steamed or baked.

Flounder

Flounder is very similar to plaice, but its flavour and texture are not so fine. It is available whole or in fillets and can be cooked in the same way as plaice. In the US, flounder is a collective name for several varieties of flat fish.

Turbot

This fish, with its huge brown, knobbly body and small head, is considered the finest of the flat fish. It is low in fat, has firm, snow-white flesh and a fine, delicate taste. Depending on its size, it is available whole, in cutlets or in fillets and can be baked, poached or steamed.

Brill

Brill is smaller but not dissimilar to turbot in flavour and texture. It is usually sold whole, but can be halved, sliced or filleted and lends itself to being cooked by any method.

Dover Sole

This is one of the finest-flavoured and finest-textured small flat fish. Its white flesh has an exquisite flavour. Available whole or in fillets, it is traditionally grilled or fried, a classic recipe being sole meunière.

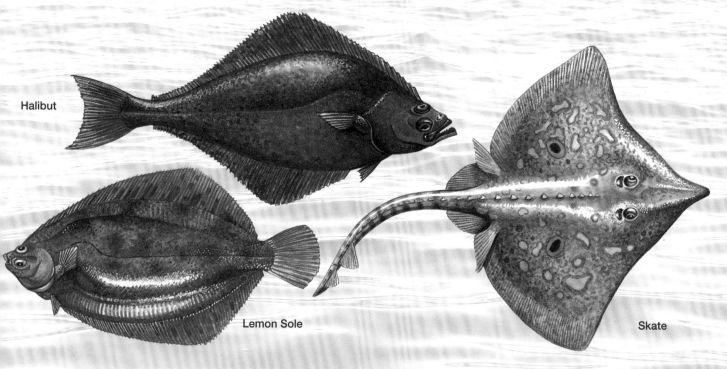

Halibut

Lemon Sole

Skate

Skate and Ray

These strange-looking fish are shaped like a kite. There are several varieties, of which only the fish's pectoral fins, known as its wings, and small pieces of flesh cut from the bony part of the fish, known as nobs, are eaten. It is low in fat and has a superior flavour. The common skate is particularly vulnerable to overfishing and is listed as endangered.

Halibut

This large flat fish is available whole or as cutlets or fillets. Its flesh is quite oily and its firm texture makes it suitable for a variety of cooking methods, including baking, braising, poaching or steaming. Halibut is vulnerable to overfishing.

Lemon Sole

Lemon sole is not dissimilar to Dover sole, although it has far less flavour, and while its white flesh has a fine texture it is less firm. It can be purchased and cooked in the same way as Dover sole.

Dab

This is one of the smallest flat fish and belongs to the plaice family. It has a rough, light brown upper skin and white flesh. It is available whole or in fillets and can be cooked in the same way as plaice.

Many species are vulnerable to overfishing – see the best choices to make in the MCS Good Fish Guide at www.mcsuk.org

Gutting & Trimming
Flat Seafish

Before preparing fish it must be cleaned. This involves removing the entrails and gills and sometimes the scales and fins. Your fish supplier should do this for you – if not, the following guidelines provide a step-by-step method.

Trimming flat seafish

If desired, using kitchen scissors, cut off the gills and fins if the fish is to be served whole. The head and tail may also be cut off using a sharp knife. Rinse the cavity under cold running water. Fins and scales obviously don't need to be removed if the fish is to be filleted or the skin is to be removed after cooking.

Gutting flat seafish

The entrails of a flat fish occupy only a small part of the fish's body cavity. To remove them, open the cavity, which lies in the upper part of the body under the gills, pull out the entrails and clean away any blood in the cavity.

Opposite: **Flounder for Two**
(see page 122)

Filleting & Skinning Flat Seafish

A very sharp knife will be required for this task, as the skin of flat fish, especially that of flounder, is quite tough.

> Filleting flat seafish

Four fillets, two from each side, are usually taken from a flat fish, although sometimes one large fillet is cut from each side – these are known as double or butterfly fillets. To make four fillets, put the fish on a chopping board with its tail towards you. Using a sharp knife, cut around the shape of the head and along the backbone from head to tail. With smooth cutting strokes, working from head to tail, separate the flesh from the bone. Turn the fish over and repeat on the other side.

> Skinning whole flat seafish

Whole flat fish are usually cooked with the skin on. However, Dover and slip soles are traditionally skinned on the dark side only before cooking.

1 Using a sharp knife, make a small cut in the dark skin across the tail.

2 Slip your thumb between the skin and flesh of the fish and loosen the skin. Then, holding the tail end firmly with one hand and gripping the skin with a cloth or kitchen paper in the other hand, pull the skin upwards towards the head. A large pinch of salt may help you to grip the flesh.

Boning Dover or Slip Sole

Dover and slip soles can be boned in preparation for stuffing. To do this, first skin both sides of the fish as described opposite under Filleting & Skinning Flat Seafish.

1 Put the fish on a chopping board with its tail towards you and, using a sharp knife, cut around the shape of the head and along the backbone from head to tail.

2 With smooth cutting strokes, working from head to tail, lift the flesh from the bone, stopping when you reach the fins. Leave the fillet completely attached to the fins, head and tail. Turn the fish around and separate the fillet on the other side of the fish in the same way.

3 Turn the fish over and repeat on the other side, leaving the fillets attached to the fins, head and tail in the same way. Using kitchen scissors, cut away all around the backbone and remove it.

Sole Meunière

Serves 2

ingredients

- 4 sole fillets, each about 175 g/6 oz, all dark skin and bones removed
- 100 ml/3½ fl oz milk
- 4 tbsp plain flour
- 85 g/3 oz butter
- juice of ½ lemon
- salt and pepper
- chopped fresh flat-leaf parsley, to garnish
- cooked asparagus and lemon wedges, to serve

1 Rinse the fish under cold running water and pat dry with kitchen paper. Pour the milk into a flat dish at least as large as the fillets and put the flour on a plate. Season each fillet on both sides with salt and pepper to taste.

2 Working with one fillet at a time, pull it very quickly through the milk, then put it in the flour, turn once to coat all over and shake off any excess flour. Continue until all the fillets are prepared.

3 Melt half the butter in a sauté pan or frying pan, large enough to hold the fillets in a single layer, over a medium–high heat. Add the fillets to the pan, skinned-side down, and fry for 2 minutes.

4 Turn over the fillets and fry for 2–3 minutes, or until the flesh flakes easily. Transfer to warmed serving plates, skinned-side up, and reserve.

5 Reduce the heat to medium and melt the remaining butter in the pan. When it stops foaming, add the lemon juice and stir, scraping the sediment from the base of the pan. Spoon the butter mixture over the fish and sprinkle with parsley. Serve with asparagus and lemon wedges.

Fillets of Sole in Tomato & Olive Sauce

Serves 4

ingredients
- 4 tbsp olive oil
- 900 g/2 lb plum tomatoes, peeled, deseeded and chopped
- 2 tbsp sun-dried tomato purée
- 3 garlic cloves, finely chopped
- 1 tbsp chopped fresh oregano
- 4 whole sole, filleted
- 85 g/3 oz plain flour
- 85 g/3 oz unsalted butter
- 115 g/4 oz black olives, stoned
- salt and pepper
- rocket leaves, to serve

1 Heat the oil in a large heavy-based saucepan. Add the tomatoes, sun-dried tomato purée, garlic and oregano, and season to taste with salt and pepper. Stir well, then cover and simmer, stirring occasionally, for 30 minutes, until the mixture is thickened and pulpy.

2 Preheat the oven to 180°C/350°F/ Gas Mark 4. Rinse the fish under cold running water and pat dry with kitchen paper. Spread out the flour on a plate and season to taste with salt and pepper. Coat the fish fillets in the seasoned flour, shaking off any excess.

3 Melt half the butter in a heavy-based frying pan. Add as many fillets as the frying pan will hold in a single layer and cook over a medium heat for 2 minutes on each side. Using a fish slice, transfer the fillets to an ovenproof dish and keep warm. Cook the remaining fillets, adding the remaining butter as required.

4 Stir the olives into the tomato sauce, then pour it over the fish. Bake in the preheated oven for 20 minutes. Transfer to warmed plates and serve immediately, accompanied by rocket leaves.

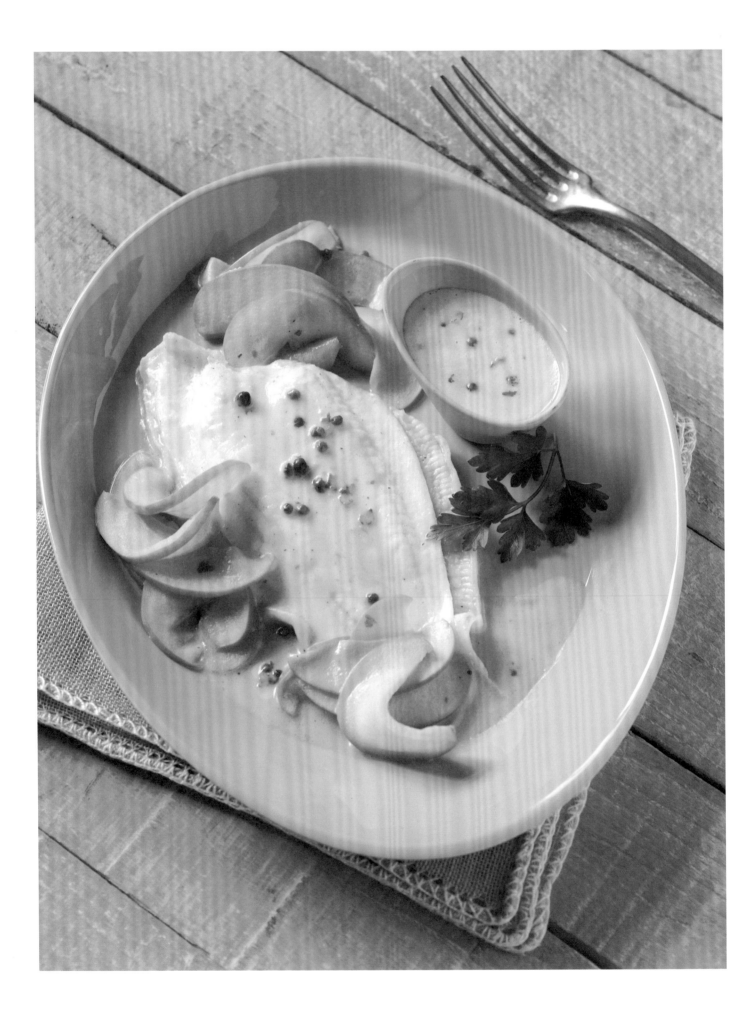

Lemon Sole with Pink Peppercorns & Apples

Serves 4

ingredients

- 8 lemon sole fillets, each about 85 g/3 oz, skinned
- 300 ml/10 fl oz fish stock (see page 20)
- 1 tbsp pink peppercorns
- 6 tbsp crème fraîche
- 3 tart green eating apples, cored and thinly sliced
- salt
- fresh flat-leaf parsley sprigs, to garnish

1 Rinse the fish under cold running water and pat dry with kitchen paper. Pour all but 3 tablespoons of the stock into a saucepan. Add the fish fillets – they usually fit better if folded in half. Bring just to the boil, then reduce the heat, cover and poach very gently for 5–8 minutes, until the flesh flakes easily.

2 Meanwhile, put the peppercorns into a separate saucepan with the remaining stock and bring to the boil over a low heat. Stir in the crème fraîche, season to taste with salt and cook, stirring frequently, for 3–5 minutes, until reduced. Add the apples and cook for 1–2 minutes, until they are soft but still firm.

3 Using a fish slice, drain the fish, reserving the cooking liquid, and transfer carefully to warmed serving plates. Using a slotted spoon, transfer the apple slices to the plates. Keep warm.

4 Bring the peppercorn mixture back to the boil and gradually stir in enough of the fish cooking liquid to make a sauce. Spoon the sauce over the fish and serve immediately, garnished with parsley sprigs.

Sole Goujons
with Tartare Sauce

Serves 4

ingredients
- 8 sole fillets, each about
  85 g/3 oz, all skin and bones
  removed
- 3–4 tbsp plain flour
- 85 g/3 oz fine fresh white
  breadcrumbs
- 2 large eggs
- sunflower oil, for deep-frying
- salt and pepper
- tartare sauce (see page 23) and
  lemon wedges, to serve

1 Rinse the fish under cold running water and pat dry with kitchen paper. Cut the fish into strips about 7.5 cm/3 inches long and 1 cm/½ inch wide, then set aside.

2 Put the flour with salt and pepper to taste in a polythene bag. Put the breadcrumbs on a plate and lightly beat the eggs with salt and pepper to taste in a large shallow bowl.

3 Heat enough oil for deep-frying in a deep-fat fryer or heavy-based saucepan to 180–190°C/350–375°F, or until a cube of bread browns in 30 seconds. Toss the fish strips in the seasoned flour, then shake off any excess flour. Quickly dip the fish strips in the egg, then coat with the breadcrumbs, making sure the fish is completely covered.

4 Drop the goujons, in batches, into the hot oil and deep-fry for 2–3 minutes, until golden and crisp. Use a slotted spoon to scoop out the goujons and drain them well on crumpled kitchen paper. Sprinkle with extra salt to taste and keep warm while frying the remaining goujons, returning the oil to the correct temperature, if necessary, before frying each batch.

5 Continue until all the fish is fried. Serve with tartare sauce on the side and lemon wedges for squeezing over.

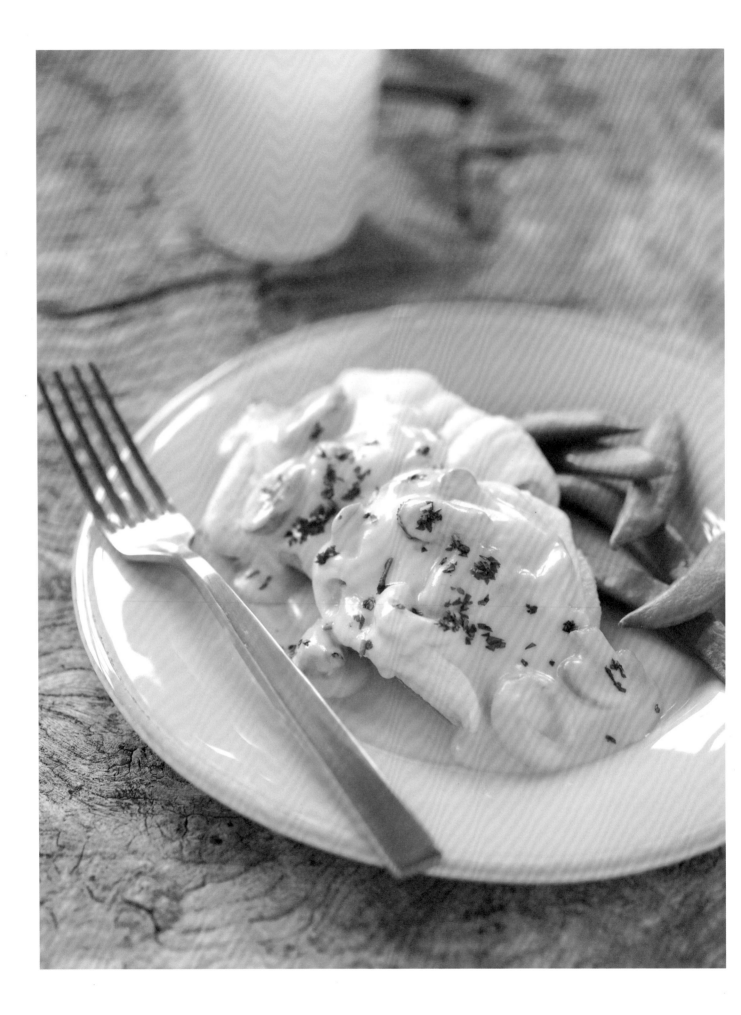

Normandy Sole

Serves 4

ingredients

- 350 g/12 oz live mussels, scrubbed and debearded
- 8 lemon sole fillets, each about 85 g/3 oz, skinned
- 300 ml/10 fl oz dry white wine
- 1 bouquet garni
- 225 g/8 oz cooked prawns, in their shells
- 2 shallots, chopped
- 85 g/3 oz unsalted butter
- 115 g/4 oz button mushrooms, thinly sliced
- 40 g/1½ oz plain flour
- 300 ml/10 fl oz double cream
- salt and pepper
- chopped fresh parsley, to garnish
- cooked sugar snap peas, to serve

1 Discard any mussels with broken shells and any that refuse to close when tapped. Rinse the fish under cold running water and pat dry with kitchen paper.

2 Put the mussels in a large saucepan, pour in the wine, add the bouquet garni and season to taste with salt and pepper.

3 Cover the pan with a tight-fitting lid and bring to the boil. Cook, shaking the pan occasionally, for 3–5 minutes, until the shells have opened. Drain the mussels, reserving the cooking liquid, and discard any that remain closed. Remove the mussels from their shells and set them aside. Discard the bouquet garni.

4 Strain the reserved cooking liquid through a muslin-lined sieve into a clean saucepan. Peel the prawns and set aside. Add the shells to the pan with the shallots. Bring to the boil over a medium heat, then reduce the heat, cover and simmer gently for 15 minutes.

5 Strain the prawn stock and return it to the saucepan. Add the fish fillets – they usually fit better if folded in half. Bring just to the boil, then reduce the heat, cover and poach very gently for 5–8 minutes, until the flesh flakes easily.

6 Meanwhile, melt half the butter in a frying pan. Add the mushrooms and cook over a low heat, stirring occasionally, for 5 minutes, until tender.

7 Using a fish slice, drain the fish, carefully transfer to a warmed serving dish and keep warm. Strain and reserve the prawn stock.

8 Melt the remaining butter in a saucepan over a low heat. Stir in the flour and cook, stirring constantly, for 2 minutes. Remove the pan from the heat and gradually stir in the cream, then the prawn stock. Return the pan to the heat and bring to the boil, stirring constantly. Reduce the heat and cook, stirring, for 2–3 minutes, until thickened and smooth. Season to taste with salt and pepper and stir in the mussels, prawns and mushrooms. Heat through gently for 2–3 minutes, then spoon the sauce over the fish. Sprinkle with parsley and serve immediately with sugar snap peas.

Flounder for Two

Serves 2

ingredients

- 1–2 whole flounder, about 1.3 kg/3 lb, gutted
- 150 ml/5 fl oz olive oil
- 375 g/13 oz waxy potatoes, peeled and thinly sliced
- 1 fennel bulb, thinly sliced
- 2 large tomatoes, grilled, peeled, deseeded and chopped
- 2 shallots, sliced
- 4 tbsp dry white wine
- salt and pepper
- chopped fresh parsley, to garnish
- lemon wedges, to serve

1 Preheat the oven to 200°C/400°F/Gas Mark 6. Rinse the fish inside and out under cold running water and pat dry with kitchen paper.

2 Spread 4 tablespoons of the oil over the base of a shallow roasting tin large enough to hold the flounder. Arrange the potatoes in a single layer, then top with the fennel, tomatoes and shallots. Season to taste with salt and pepper. Drizzle with a further 4 tablespoons of the oil. Roast the vegetables in the preheated oven for 30 minutes.

3 Season the fish to taste with salt and pepper and put on top of the vegetables. Sprinkle with the wine and the remaining oil.

4 Return the roasting tin to the oven and roast the fish, uncovered, for 20 minutes, or until the flesh flakes easily.

5 To serve, cut each fish into 4 fillets or 2 double fillets. Divide the vegetables between two serving plates and place the fish fillets on top. Sprinkle over the parsley and serve immediately, accompanied by lemon wedges for squeezing over.

Nut-crusted Halibut

Serves 4

ingredients
- 750 g/1 lb 10 oz halibut fillet
- 40 g/1½ oz butter, melted
- 55 g/2 oz pistachio nuts, shelled and roughly chopped
- mixed salad and lemon wedges, to serve

1 Rinse the fish under cold running water and pat dry with kitchen paper. Brush the melted butter over the halibut fillet.

2 Spread out the nuts on a large plate. Roll the fish in the nuts, pressing down gently.

3 Preheat a griddle pan over a medium heat. Cook the halibut, turning once, for 10 minutes, or until firm but tender – the exact cooking time will depend on the thickness of the fillet.

4 Remove the fish and any loose pistachio pieces from the heat and transfer to warmed serving plates. Serve immediately, accompanied by mixed salad and lemon wedges.

Grilled Halibut
with Garlic Butter

Serves 4

ingredients

- 4 halibut fillets, each about 175 g/6 oz
- 75 g/2¾ oz butter, plus extra for greasing
- 2 garlic cloves, finely chopped
- salt and pepper
- fresh flat-leaf parsley sprigs, to garnish
- cooked French beans and lime wedges, to serve

1 Preheat the grill to medium. Rinse the fish under cold running water and pat dry with kitchen paper.

2 Grease a shallow heatproof dish with butter, then arrange the fish in it. Season to taste with salt and pepper.

3 In a separate bowl, mix the butter with the garlic. Arrange pieces of the garlic butter all over the fish, then transfer to the preheated grill. Cook for 7–8 minutes, turning once, until the fish is cooked through.

4 Remove the dish from the grill. Using a fish slice, remove the fillets from the dish and arrange on individual serving plates. Pour over the melted butter from the dish and garnish with parsley sprigs. Serve with French beans and lime wedges.

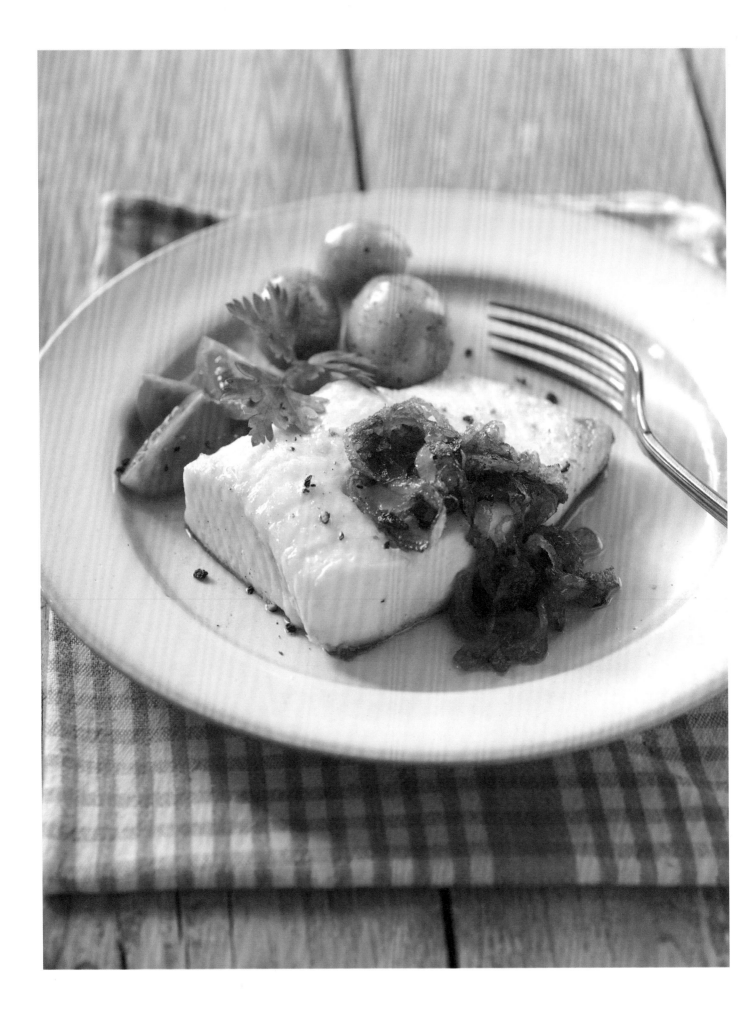

Grilled Halibut
with Caramelized Onion

Serves 2

ingredients
- 1 tbsp vegetable oil
- 1 small onion, thinly sliced
- 1 tsp balsamic vinegar
- 2 halibut fillets or steaks, each about 115 g/4 oz
- 2 tbsp melted butter
- fresh flat-leaf parsley sprigs, to garnish
- cooked new potatoes and tomato wedges, to serve

1 Heat the oil in a large frying pan over a medium heat. Add the onion, stir well and reduce the heat. Cook over a very low heat, stirring occasionally, for 15–20 minutes, until the onion is very soft and brown.

2 Add the vinegar to the pan and cook, stirring constantly to prevent sticking, for 2 minutes.

3 Rinse the fish under cold running water and pat dry with kitchen paper. Brush the melted butter over the fish.

4 Preheat the grill to hot. Sear the fish, then reduce the heat and cook for about 10 minutes, turning once. The cooking time will depend on the thickness of the fillets, but the fish should be firm and tender when done.

5 Remove the fish from the heat, transfer to warmed serving plates and top with the caramelized onion. Garnish with parsley sprigs and serve with new potatoes and tomato wedges.

Pan-fried Halibut Steaks
with Tomato Salsa

Serves 4

ingredients
- 4 halibut steaks, each about 2.5 cm/1 inch thick
- 1 tbsp vegetable oil
- 50 g/1¾ oz butter
- flour, for dusting
- juice of ½ lemon
- salt and pepper

tomato salsa
- 3 firm tomatoes, halved, deseeded and finely diced
- 1 small red onion, finely diced
- 1 fresh green chilli, deseeded and finely chopped
- 3 tbsp chopped fresh coriander
- juice of 1 lime
- ½ tsp sea salt

1 Rinse the fish under cold running water and pat dry with kitchen paper.

2 Combine all the salsa ingredients in a serving bowl and leave to stand at room temperature.

3 Heat the oil and 40 g/1½ oz of the butter in a large frying pan over a medium–high heat. Dust the halibut steaks with flour and season to taste with salt and pepper. Place in the pan and cook for 5 minutes on one side, then turn over and cook for 3–4 minutes on the other side, until golden and cooked through. Transfer to a warmed serving dish.

4 Add the lemon juice to the pan and simmer over a medium heat for a few seconds, scraping up any sediment from the base of the pan. Stir in the remaining butter and cook for a few seconds. Pour over the fish and serve immediately with the salsa.

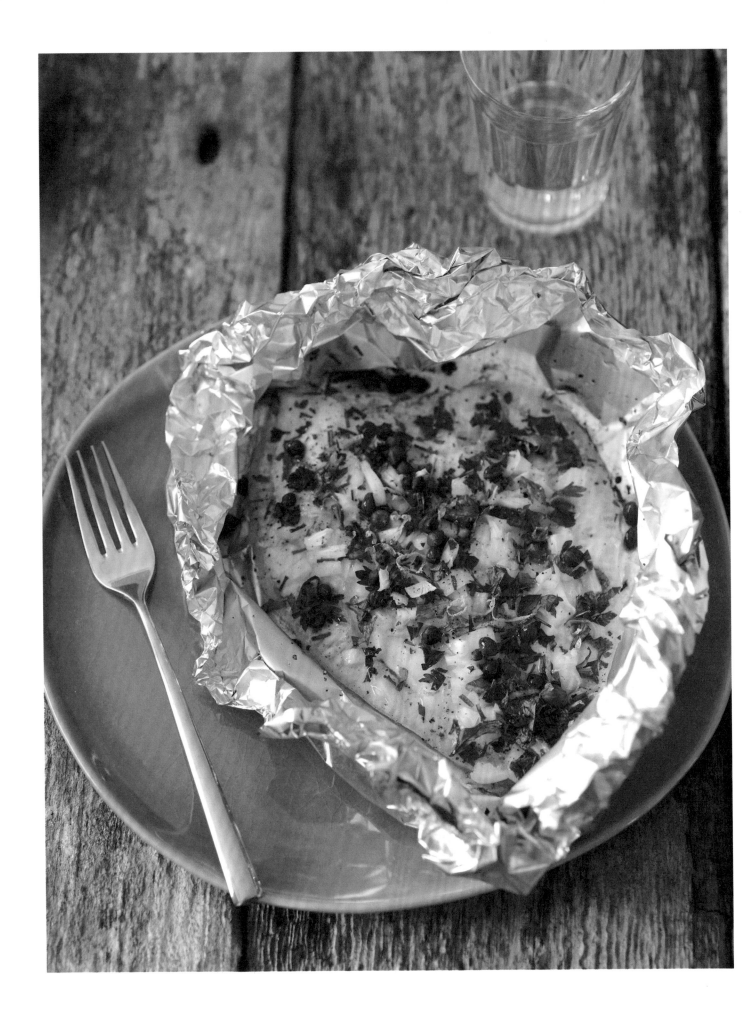

Plaice Parcels
with Fresh Herbs

Serves 4

ingredients

- vegetable oil, for brushing
- 4 plaice fillets, skinned
- 6 tbsp chopped fresh herbs, such as dill, parsley, chives, thyme or marjoram
- grated rind and juice of 2 lemons
- 1 small onion, finely chopped
- 1 tbsp capers (optional)
- salt and pepper

1 Preheat the oven to 190°C/375°F/ Gas Mark 5. Cut four large squares of aluminium foil, each large enough to hold a fish fillet and form a parcel, and brush with oil.

2 Rinse the fish under cold running water and pat dry with kitchen paper. Place each fish fillet on a foil square and sprinkle over the herbs, lemon rind and juice, onion, capers, if using, and salt and pepper to taste.

3 Fold the foil to enclose each fish fillet and make a secure parcel and place on a baking tray.

4 Bake the parcels in the preheated oven for 15 minutes, or until cooked through and tender.

5 Transfer to individual serving plates and unwrap the parcels. Serve immediately.

Plaice with Egg & Dill Sauce

Serves 4

ingredients
- 4 plaice fillets, each about 225 g/8 oz
- 85 g/3 oz butter, plus extra for greasing
- juice of ½ lemon
- 4 hard-boiled eggs, finely chopped, plus extra halves to garnish
- 4 cornichons or other small gherkins, finely chopped
- 2 tbsp chopped fresh dill, plus extra sprigs to garnish
- salt and pepper

1 Preheat the grill to medium. Rinse the fish under cold running water and pat dry with kitchen paper. Generously grease a baking tray with butter and put the fish fillets on it, skin-side down.

2 Melt the butter in a saucepan over a low heat. Remove the pan from the heat and brush some of the butter over the fish. Set the remainder aside. Season the fish with salt and pepper to taste, place under the preheated grill and cook, without turning, for 8 minutes, until the flesh flakes easily.

3 Just before the fish is cooked, stir the lemon juice, the chopped hard-boiled eggs, cornichons and chopped dill into the remaining melted butter. Heat gently, stirring occasionally, for 2 minutes.

4 Using a fish slice, transfer the fish fillets to warmed serving plates. Spoon over the sauce, garnish with dill sprigs and hard-boiled egg halves, and serve immediately.

Plaice Roasted with Lime

Serves 4

ingredients
- 4 plaice fillets, each about 250 g/9 oz
- juice of 1 lime
- 3 tbsp extra virgin olive oil
- 1 large onion, finely chopped
- 3 garlic cloves, finely chopped
- 2–3 pickled jalapeño chillies (jalapeños en escabeche), chopped
- 6–8 tbsp chopped fresh coriander, plus extra sprigs to garnish
- salt and pepper
- lime wedges, to serve

1 Preheat the oven to 180°C/350°F/ Gas Mark 4.

2 Rinse the fish under cold running water and pat dry with kitchen paper. Place the fish fillets in a non-metallic bowl and season to taste with salt and pepper. Sprinkle the lime juice over the fish.

3 Heat the oil in a frying pan. Add the onion and garlic and cook, stirring frequently, for 2 minutes, or until softened. Remove the frying pan from the heat.

4 Place a third of the onion mixture and a little of the chillies and chopped coriander in the base of a shallow ovenproof dish or roasting tin. Arrange the fish on top. Top with the remaining onion mixture, chillies and chopped coriander.

5 Roast in the preheated oven for 15–20 minutes, or until the fish has become slightly opaque and firm to the touch. Garnish with coriander sprigs and serve immediately with lime wedges for squeezing over.

Plaice with a Fluffy
Cheese Topping

Serves 4

ingredients
- 900 g/2 lb plaice fillets
- 55 g/2 oz unsalted butter, plus extra for greasing
- 1 red pepper, deseeded and thinly sliced
- 600 ml/1 pint mayonnaise (see page 22)
- 225 g/8 oz Cheddar cheese, grated
- 4 tbsp double cream
- 4 egg whites
- salt and pepper
- fresh watercress sprigs, to garnish

1 Preheat the oven to 180°C/350°F/ Gas Mark 4. Rinse the fish under cold running water and pat dry with kitchen paper. Grease a large ovenproof dish with butter.

2 Melt the butter in a large heavy-based frying pan. Add the fish fillets, in batches, and cook over a medium heat for 2 minutes on each side. Using a fish slice, transfer the fish to a chopping board and carefully remove and discard the skin, then put the fillets in the prepared dish. Sprinkle the red pepper on top.

3 Mix together the mayonnaise, cheese and cream in a bowl and season to taste with salt and pepper. Whisk the egg whites in a grease-free bowl until stiff but not dry. Gently fold the egg whites into the mayonnaise mixture.

4 Pour the mayonnaise mixture over the fish to cover it completely. Place the dish on a baking tray and bake in the preheated oven for 20 minutes, until the topping is fluffy and lightly browned. Serve immediately, garnished with watercress.

Chapter 4
Shellfish

The Shellfish Directory

The following is a guide to all the main species of edible shellfish, listed by their common names, although some are known by a variety of different names. The potted profile for each fish details the various forms in which it can be purchased, for example live or cooked, fresh or canned, frozen or smoked, and the most suitable cooking methods.

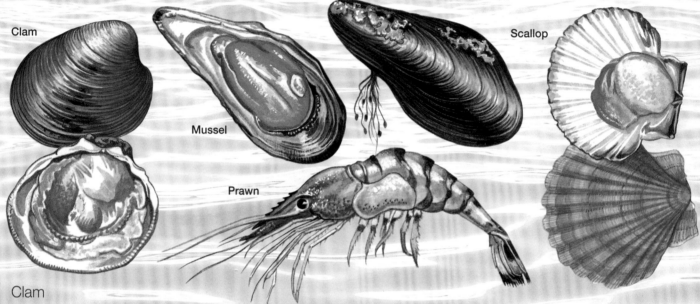

Clam

Mussel

Scallop

Prawn

Clam

There are many varieties of clam, which vary in size and have either soft or hard shells. They are sold live in their shells and larger clams are steamed open, whereas smaller varieties can be eaten raw. They are also sold smoked and canned.

Mussel

Identified by their dark blue shell, mussels cling to rocks or the sea bed and take about two years to reach maturity. They are available live or frozen and are cooked by steaming, which opens their shells.

Oyster

There are many varieties of this shellfish, which vary in size. The traditional way of eating them is raw, straight from the half shell, with their juices. Shucked (shelled) oysters are available smoked, canned and dried.

Scallop & Queen

Scallops and queens both have ribbed fan shells, but queen scallops, or queenies, are smaller than scallops and are more widely available. Unlike other molluscs, scallops

cannot hold their shells tightly closed and die soon after they are taken out of water. This means that they are very perishable and are often removed from their shells and iced aboard fishing boats as soon as they are caught. Both the white muscle and orange coral, or roe, are eaten and have an exquisite, delicate taste. They can be bought fresh or frozen and can be fried, grilled or steamed.

Shrimp

This is the smallest crustacean, of which there are several varieties, such as the brown, pink and deep-water shrimp. Like prawns, they are translucent when alive and turn pink when cooked. Shrimps are mainly sold frozen, but are also available canned, salted and dried.

Prawn

This shellfish is larger than the shrimp and is also available cooked whole or peeled and frozen, canned or dried.

Lobster

Lobster, considered by some to be the finest crustacean, can take seven years to reach marketable size. There are several

Many species are vulnerable to overfishing – see the best choices to make in the MCS Good Fish Guide at www.mcsuk.org

Crab

Lobster

Squid

varieties and they can be bought live, when dark blue, or cooked in the shell, when the lobster turns bright pink. Lobster can also be purchased frozen whole or as frozen tails, and canned. It can be baked, boiled, steamed or grilled.

Dublin Bay Prawn/Langoustine/Norway Lobster/Scampi

This shellfish looks like a miniature version of a lobster. It is available live or cooked, with its shell or peeled. When peeled and coated in breadcrumbs, it is known as scampi.

Rock Lobster/Spiny Lobster

This is another shellfish that looks similar to a small lobster. It is prepared and cooked in the same way as lobster.

Freshwater Crayfish

Also resembling a tiny lobster, these are the only shellfish found in fresh waters.

Crab

There are several varieties of this crustacean, including the blue or soft-shell crab, the common crab, the green

or shore crab and the spider crab. Crab can be bought live, uncooked in the shell, cooked, with or without the shell, fresh and canned. Its flesh consists of white meat, found in the claws and legs, and brown meat, found in the body. Crab can be baked, steamed or boiled. Fresh crab can also be purchased 'dressed', with the meat arranged attractively in the shell ready for eating. Canned dressed crab is also available.

Octopus

The octopus is a cephalopod and has eight tentacles. It varies in size and large ones – as large as 3 metres/10 feet – are available prepared in pieces and small ones are available whole. Octopus can be poached or used in soups and stews.

Squid

The squid, of which there are several varieties varying in size, is a cephalopod and has ten tentacles. The tentacles are chopped and the body either sliced or kept whole and stuffed. Large squid are usually stewed and small squid can be fried, grilled or poached. The ink, found in a sac, can also be used in cooking. Squid is available fresh or frozen.

Preparing Cephalopods

Although it may seem a bit daunting, there is no great mystery about cleaning and gutting cephalopods, although great care must be taken not to pierce the ink sacs. The step-by-step procedure described below will help to demystify the process.

> Preparing squid

Put the squid on a chopping board and, grasping the body in one hand, gently pull off the head and tentacles with the other hand. The body entrails will come away at the same time and should be discarded.

> Preparing octopus

Put the octopus on a chopping board and, grasping the body in one hand, firmly pull off the head and tentacles with the other hand. The body entrails will come away at the same time and should be discarded along with the ink sac. Cut off the edible tentacles just in front of the eyes. Rinse the body and tentacles under cold running water and dry on kitchen paper, then beat well with a rolling pin or wooden meat mallet to tenderize the flesh.

1 Cut off the edible tentacles just in front of the eyes and reserve, then squeeze out the small hard beak and discard.

2 Remove the transparent quill that runs along the length of the body of the squid.

3 Carefully remove one or two of the ink sacs from the head so that you do not pierce them, and reserve them if you want to use the ink in another recipe. Discard the head.

4 Rub off the thin, dark, outer membrane with your fingers. Rinse under cold running water and dry on kitchen paper.

Preparing Shellfish

Buying live shellfish and preparing them at home yourself is actually quite simple if you follow the steps described below. Doing your own preparation will also ensure that when the fish reaches your table it is as fresh as possible.

> Preparing crab

Crab is usually sold cooked, but should you buy a live one, the most humane way of killing it is to put it into the freezer for 2 hours to put it to sleep before boiling it, covered, in a saucepan of heavily salted water for 15 minutes, allowing an extra 10 minutes for each additional crab. Leave the crab to cool in the water.

1 To prepare a cooked crab, have two bowls ready, one for white meat and one for brown meat. Put the crab on its back on a chopping board. Gripping a claw firmly in one hand and as close to the body as possible, twist it off. Remove the other claw and the legs in the same way.

2 Break the claws in half by bending them backwards at the joint. Crack the shells of the claws and larger legs with a rolling pin and remove the white meat with a skewer or teaspoon handle. Reserve the small legs for garnishing.

3 Put the crab on its back with its eyes and mouth facing away from you. Remove the stomach sac and mouth, which are attached to the back shell, and discard them.

4 Gripping the shell firmly, press the body section upwards and gently pull them apart. Remove the soft grey gills that are attached along the edges of the body and discard.

5 Cut the body into two or four pieces and carefully pick out the flesh. Scoop out the brown meat from the shell.

> Preparing lobster

A live lobster should be cooked in the same way as a crab (see page 146), but when you remove it from the freezer, weigh it quickly before plunging it into the water. Calculate the cooking time by allowing 18 minutes for the first 500 g/1 lb 2 oz and an extra 11 minutes for every additional 500 g/1 lb 2 oz.

1 To prepare a cooked lobster, put it on a chopping board and twist off the claws and pincers. Crack open the large claws and remove the flesh, discarding the membrane. The small claws can be reserved for garnishing.

2 Using the point of a sharp knife, split the shell of the lobster in half from head to tail.

3 Remove the flesh from the tail, reserving the coral (only found in females and at certain times of the year), and, using a skewer, scrape out the flesh from the back legs.

4 Remove and discard the thread-like intestine, the stomach sac and the spongy gills.

> Preparing prawns

1 To peel a prawn, hold its head between your thumb and forefinger and, using the fingers of your other hand, hold the tail and gently pinch and pull off the tail shell.

2 Holding the body, pull off the head, body shell and claws.

3 To devein a prawn, using the point of a sharp knife or skewer, carefully pull out the dark vein that runs down the prawn's back and discard.

> Preparing oysters

1 Scrub each oyster shell with a stiff scrubbing brush under cold running water.

2 Hold each oyster, with the rounded side down, in a clean tea towel. Using a strong, short knife or, ideally, a shucking knife, insert the knife at the hinge and prise the shell upwards to open. Take great care when doing this.

3 Slide the knife along the inside of the upper shell to cut the muscle and release the oyster. Try to reserve as much of the juice as possible. Oysters served raw 'on the half shell' are served with their juices in the bottom shell.

> Preparing clams

Scrub each clam with a stiff scrubbing brush under cold running water to clean the shell, then put on a chopping board or hold each clam in a cloth in the palm of your hand and prise the shell open at the hinge with a knife, ideally a clam knife. If the clams are very difficult to open, they can be helped by putting them on a baking tray in a very hot oven for 4–5 minutes, until they begin to open.

Loosen the clams and leave each in one half of the shell if you are intending to serve them raw. Reserve any juice from the clams, as this can be strained and used in a sauce. It should certainly not be discarded.

> Preparing scallops

1 Scrub each scallop shell with a stiff scrubbing brush under cold running water to remove as much sand as possible.

2 Discard any scallops that are open and will not close when tapped sharply with the back of a knife. Using a strong knife, prise the shell open. If the scallops are very difficult to open, they can be helped by putting them on a baking tray, rounded side uppermost,

in a very hot oven for 4–5 minutes, until the shells begin to open.

3 Remove and discard the grey beard that surrounds each scallop as well as the black thread and stomach bag. Detach the scallop and coral from the shell with a spoon. Rinse under cold running water and dry on kitchen paper.

> Preparing mussels

Clean each mussel by scrubbing or scraping the shell under cold running water to remove any barnacles, mud or seaweed. Pull away any beards that are attached to the mussel shells. It is the beard that the mussel uses to cling to the rocks so you will need to tug hard. If the mussel is open and will not close when tapped sharply with the back of a knife, it is dead and should be discarded.

Also discard any mussels with broken shells and any that feel particularly heavy, as these are probably filled with sand. Put the mussels in a colander, rinse well under cold running water, then drain well.

Bouillabaisse

Serves 4

ingredients
- 200 g/7 oz live mussels, scrubbed and debearded
- 100 ml/3½ fl oz olive oil
- 3 garlic cloves, chopped
- 2 onions, chopped
- 2 tomatoes, deseeded and chopped
- 700 ml/1¼ pints fish stock (see page 20)
- 400 ml/14 fl oz white wine
- 1 bay leaf
- pinch of saffron threads
- 2 tbsp chopped fresh basil
- 2 tbsp chopped fresh parsley
- 250 g/9 oz snapper or monkfish fillets
- 250 g/9 oz haddock fillets, skinned
- 200 g/7 oz raw prawns, peeled and deveined
- 100 g/3½ oz prepared scallops
- salt and pepper
- fresh crusty bread, to serve

1 Discard any mussels with broken shells and any that refuse to close when tapped. Put the remainder into a large pan with a little water, bring to the boil and cook over a high heat for 4 minutes. Transfer the cooked mussels to a bowl, discarding any that remain closed, and reserve. Wipe out the pan with kitchen paper.

2 Heat the oil in the pan over a medium heat. Add the garlic and onions and cook, stirring, for 3 minutes. Stir in the tomatoes, stock, wine, bay leaf, saffron and herbs. Bring to the boil, reduce the heat, cover and simmer for 30 minutes.

3 When the tomato mixture is cooked, rinse the fish under cold running water, pat dry with kitchen paper and cut into chunks. Add to the pan and simmer for 5 minutes. Add the mussels, prawns and scallops, and season to taste with salt and pepper. Cook for 3 minutes, until the fish is cooked through.

4 Remove from the heat, discard the bay leaf and ladle into serving bowls. Serve immediately with crusty bread.

Mussels with Herb & Garlic Butter

Serves 8

ingredients
- 800 g/1 lb 12 oz live mussels, scrubbed and debearded
- splash of dry white wine
- 1 bay leaf
- 85 g/3 oz butter
- 35 g/1¼ oz fresh white or brown breadcrumbs
- 4 tbsp chopped fresh flat-leaf parsley
- 2 tbsp snipped fresh chives
- 2 garlic cloves, finely chopped
- salt and pepper
- lemon wedges, to serve

1 Preheat the oven to 230°C/450°F/Gas Mark 8.

2 Discard any mussels with broken shells and any that refuse to close when tapped. Put the remainder in a large saucepan and add the wine and bay leaf. Cook, covered, over a high heat, shaking the saucepan occasionally, for 3–4 minutes, or until the mussels have opened. Discard any that remain closed. Strain the mussels.

3 Remove and discard the top (empty) shells from the mussels. Arrange the mussels, in their half shells, in a large ovenproof dish.

4 Melt the butter in a small saucepan and pour into a small bowl. Add the breadcrumbs, parsley, chives, garlic, and salt and pepper to taste and mix together well. Leave until the butter has set slightly. Using your fingers or two teaspoons, take a large pinch of the butter mixture and use to fill each mussel shell, pressing it down well.

5 Bake the mussels in the preheated oven for 10 minutes, or until hot. Serve immediately, accompanied by lemon wedges for squeezing over.

Moules Marinière

Serves 4

ingredients

- 2 kg/4 lb 8 oz live mussels, scrubbed and debearded
- 300 ml/10 fl oz dry white wine
- 6 shallots, finely chopped
- 1 bouquet garni
- pepper
- fresh flat-leaf parsley sprigs, to garnish
- fresh crusty bread, to serve

1 Discard any mussels with broken shells and any that refuse to close when tapped.

2 Pour the wine into a large heavy-based saucepan, add the shallots and bouquet garni and season to taste with pepper. Bring to the boil over a medium heat, add the mussels and cover tightly. Cook, shaking the saucepan occasionally, for 3–4 minutes, or until the mussels have opened. Remove and discard the bouquet garni and any mussels that remain closed.

3 Using a slotted spoon, divide the mussels among individual serving dishes. Tilt the saucepan to let any sand settle, then spoon the cooking liquid over the mussels. Garnish with parsley sprigs and serve immediately with crusty bread.

Scallops with Pea Purée

Serves 4

ingredients
- 500 g/1 lb 2 oz frozen petits pois, or peas
- 2 large handfuls of fresh mint leaves, roughly chopped
- 150 g/5½ oz butter
- 12 prepared scallops, with corals
- salt and pepper
- extra virgin olive oil, for drizzling

1 Bring a large saucepan of water to the boil, then add the petits pois. Bring back to the boil and simmer for 3 minutes. Drain the petits pois, then put them in a food processor with the mint, 100 g/3½ oz of the butter and a large pinch of salt. Blend to a smooth purée, adding a little hot water if the mixture needs loosening. Taste and adjust the seasoning, adding salt and pepper if needed, cover and keep warm.

2 Pat the scallops dry with kitchen paper, then season them well with salt and pepper. Place a large frying pan over a high heat and add the remaining butter. When the butter starts to smoke, add the scallops and sear them for 1–2 minutes on each side. They should be brown and crisp on the outside but light and moist in the middle. Remove the pan from the heat.

3 Spoon a little of the pea purée onto each of four warmed serving plates and place the scallops on top. Drizzle over a little extra virgin olive oil and serve immediately.

Seared Scallops with Leeks

Serves 4

ingredients

- 4 thin leeks, halved lengthways then crossways
- 5 tbsp olive oil
- 20 large prepared scallops, corals removed
- salt and pepper
- snipped fresh chives, to garnish
- lemon wedges, to serve

1 Preheat the oven to 230°C/450°F/ Gas Mark 8. Arrange the leeks, cut-side up, in a single layer in an ovenproof dish. Drizzle with 3 tablespoons of the oil, then sprinkle with salt and pepper to taste, pushing it into the crevices. Cook in the preheated oven for 8–10 minutes, until the leeks are brown at the edges but still bright green and tender-crisp.

2 Pat the scallops dry with kitchen paper, then score them with criss-cross slashes. Heat the remaining oil in a frying pan over a high heat. Cook the scallops for 1–2 minutes on each side, until just browned but slightly translucent on the inside.

3 Remove the leeks from the oven and arrange on warmed serving plates with the scallops on top. Simmer the scallop juices in the pan until slightly reduced, then pour over the scallops and leeks. Garnish with chives and serve immediately with lemon wedges.

Clam Chowder

Serves 8

ingredients

- 1 tbsp sunflower oil
- 115 g/4 oz bacon, diced
- 40 g/1½ oz butter
- 2 onions, chopped
- 3 potatoes, diced
- 3 celery sticks, chopped
- 3 leeks, sliced
- 600 g/1 lb 5 oz canned chopped tomatoes
- 4 tbsp chopped fresh parsley
- 1.7 litres/3 pints fish stock (see page 20)
- 1.25 kg/2 lb 12 oz live carpet shell or Venus clams
- 300 ml/10 fl oz water
- salt and pepper
- fresh crusty bread, to serve

1 Heat the oil in a large saucepan over a medium heat. Add the bacon and cook over a low–medium heat, stirring frequently, for 6–8 minutes, until crisp. Remove with a slotted spoon and set aside.

2 Melt the butter in a pan. Add the onions, potatoes and celery, then season to taste with salt. Reduce the heat to low, cover and cook, stirring occasionally, for 10 minutes, until thoroughly softened but not coloured. Add the leeks, tomatoes and 3 tablespoons of the parsley. Pour in the stock, stir well and bring to the boil over a medium heat. Reduce the heat, cover and simmer gently for 10 minutes, until the vegetables are tender.

3 Meanwhile, scrub the clams under cold running water and discard any with broken shells and any that refuse to close when tapped. Put them into a separate saucepan and pour in the water. Cover and cook over a high heat, shaking the pan occasionally, for 4–5 minutes, until the shells open.

4 Remove the clams with a slotted spoon and discard any that remain closed. Strain the cooking liquid through a muslin-lined strainer into the chowder. Remove the clams from their shells.

5 Season the chowder to taste with salt and pepper and stir in the clams. Ladle the chowder into warmed serving dishes, then sprinkle with the bacon and the remaining parsley and serve with crusty bread.

Linguine with Clams

Serves 4

ingredients
- 1 kg/2 lb 4 oz live clams
- 200 g/7 oz dried linguine
- 3 tbsp extra virgin olive oil
- 4 garlic cloves, finely chopped
- 2 shallots, finely chopped
- ½ fresh red chilli, finely chopped
- 125 ml/4 fl oz white wine
- handful of fresh parsley, chopped
- grated rind of 1 lemon
- salt and pepper

1 Scrub the clams under cold running water. Discard any with broken shells and any that refuse to close when tapped.

2 Bring a large saucepan of lightly salted water to the boil. Add the pasta and cook for about 8–10 minutes, until tender but still firm to the bite. Drain.

3 Meanwhile, add half the oil to a large saucepan and place over a high heat. Add the garlic, shallots and chilli, and cook gently for 8–10 minutes, until soft.

4 Add the wine, bring to the boil and cook for 2 minutes. Add the clams, cover and cook for a further 2–5 minutes, or until the clams have opened. Discard any that remain closed.

5 Add the drained linguine, parsley, lemon rind, the remaining oil, and salt and pepper to taste and mix through. Transfer to warmed serving dishes and serve immediately.

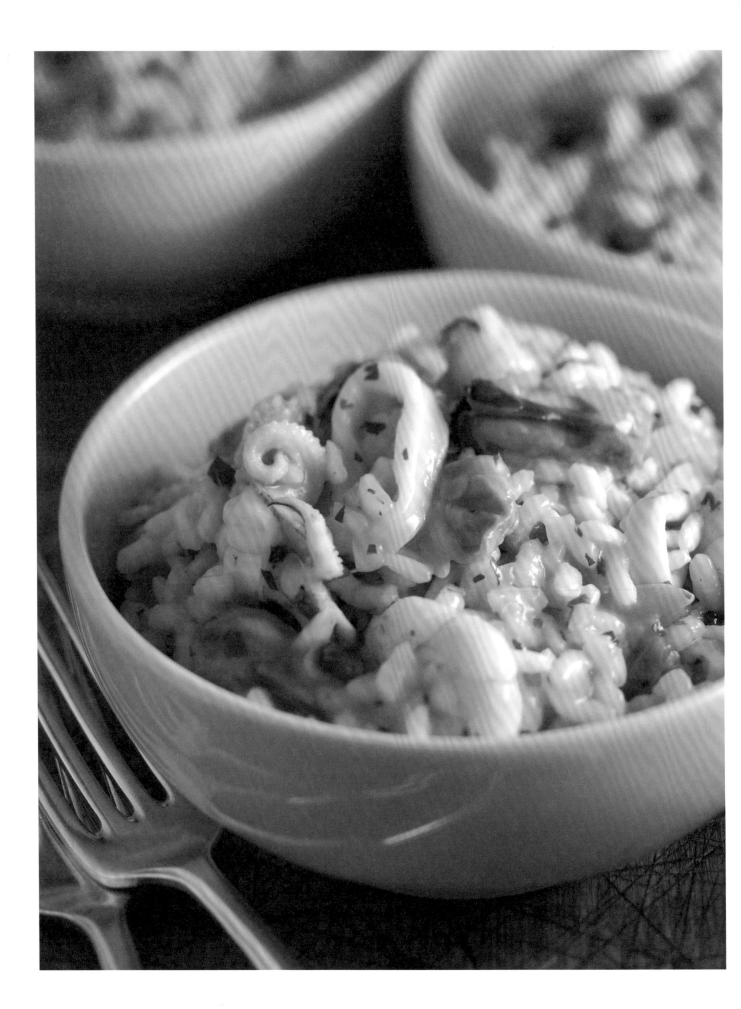

Seafood Risotto

Serves 4

ingredients

- 225 g/8 oz live mussels, scrubbed and debearded
- 225 g/8 oz live clams, scrubbed
- 2 garlic cloves, halved
- 1 lemon, sliced
- 600 ml/1 pint water
- 115 g/4 oz butter
- 1 tbsp olive oil
- 1 onion, finely chopped
- 2 tbsp chopped fresh flat-leaf parsley
- 350 g/12 oz risotto rice
- 125 ml/4 fl oz dry white wine
- 225 g /8 oz prepared squid, cut into small pieces or rings, rinsed and patted dry
- 225 g/8 oz large raw prawns, peeled and deveined
- 4 tbsp Marsala
- salt and pepper

1 Discard any mussels and clams with broken shells and any that refuse to close when tapped.

2 Place the garlic, lemon, mussels and clams in a saucepan. Pour in the water, cover tightly and bring to the boil. Cook, shaking frequently, for 5 minutes, until the shellfish have opened. Discard any that remain closed.

3 Remove the clams and mussels from their shells and set aside. Strain the cooking liquid, then make up to 1.2 litres/ 2 pints with water and pour into a saucepan. Bring to the boil, then reduce the heat and keep simmering gently over a low heat while you make the risotto.

4 Melt 25 g/1 oz of the butter with the oil in a deep saucepan. Add the onion and half the parsley and cook over a medium heat, stirring occasionally, for 5 minutes, or until softened. Reduce the heat, add the rice and cook, stirring constantly, for 2–3 minutes, or until the grains are translucent. Add the wine and cook, stirring constantly, for 1 minute, until reduced.

5 Gradually add the hot stock, a ladleful at a time. Stir constantly and add more liquid as the rice absorbs each addition. Cook for 20 minutes, or until all the liquid has been absorbed and the rice is creamy but still firm to the bite.

6 Meanwhile, melt 55 g/2 oz of the remaining butter in a separate saucepan. Add the squid and cook, stirring frequently, for 3 minutes, then add the prawns and cook for a further 2–3 minutes, until the squid is opaque and the prawns have changed colour. Stir in the Marsala, bring to the boil and cook until all the liquid has evaporated.

7 Stir the squid, prawns, mussels and clams into the risotto with the remaining butter and parsley. Season to taste with salt and pepper. Heat through briefly and serve immediately.

Oysters Rockefeller

Serves 4

ingredients
- 24 large live oysters
- rock salt
- 40 g/1½ oz butter
- 6 spring onions, chopped
- 1 large garlic clove, crushed
- 3 tbsp finely chopped celery
- 40 g/1½ oz watercress sprigs
- 85 g/3 oz baby spinach leaves, rinsed and any tough stems removed
- 1 tbsp aniseed-flavoured liqueur
- 4 tbsp fresh breadcrumbs
- a few drops of hot pepper sauce, to taste
- salt and pepper
- lemon wedges, to serve

1 Preheat the oven to 200°C/400°F/ Gas Mark 6. Shuck the oysters, running an oyster knife under each oyster to loosen it from its shell. Pour off the liquor.

2 Arrange a 1–2-cm/½–¾-inch layer of rock salt in a roasting tin large enough to hold the oysters in a single layer, or use 2 roasting tins. Nestle the oyster shells in the salt so that they remain upright. Cover with a damp tea towel and leave to chill while you make the topping.

3 Melt half the butter in a large frying pan over a medium heat. Add the spring onions, garlic and celery and cook, stirring frequently, for 2–3 minutes, until softened.

4 Stir in the remaining butter, then add the watercress and spinach and cook, stirring constantly, for 1 minute, or until the leaves wilt. Transfer to a blender or small food processor and add the liqueur, breadcrumbs, hot pepper sauce, and salt and pepper to taste. Process until well blended.

5 Spoon 2–3 teaspoons of the sauce over each oyster. Bake in the preheated oven for 20 minutes. Transfer to serving plates and serve with lemon wedges.

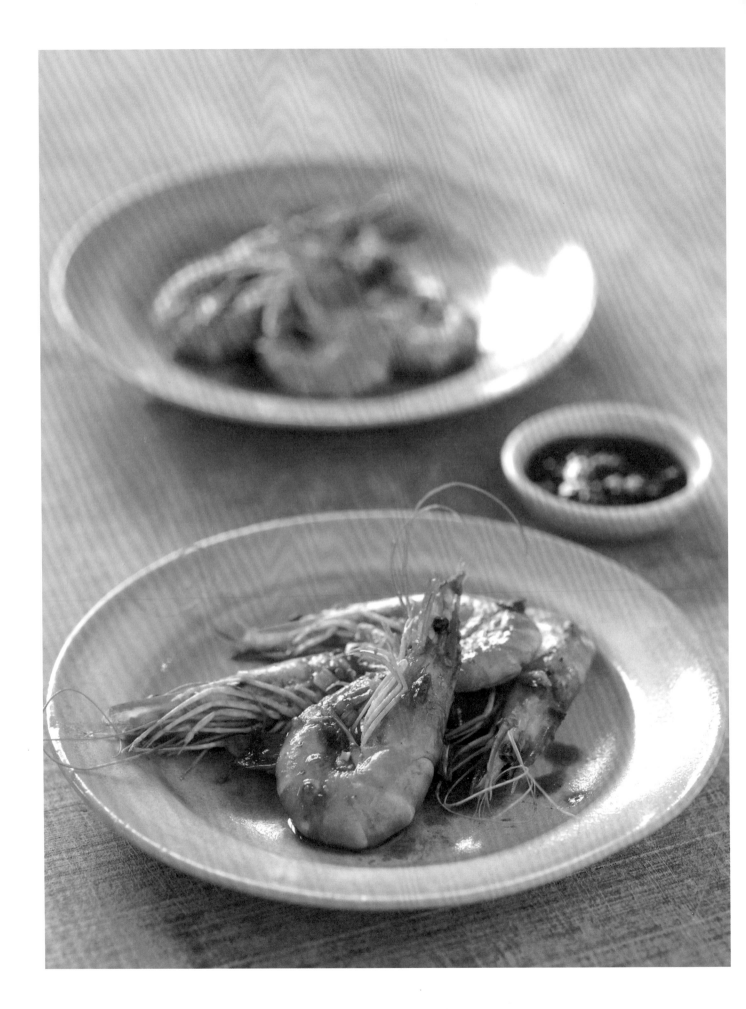

Wok-fried King Prawns
in Spicy Sauce

Serves 4

ingredients

- 3 tbsp vegetable or groundnut oil
- 450 g/1 lb raw king prawns, in their shells
- 2 tsp finely chopped fresh ginger
- 1 tsp finely chopped garlic
- 1 tbsp chopped spring onion
- 2 tbsp chilli bean sauce
- 1 tsp Shaoxing rice wine
- 1 tsp sugar
- ½ tsp light soy sauce
- 1–2 tbsp chicken stock

1 Preheat a wok, then add the oil and heat. Toss in the prawns and stir-fry over a high heat for about 4 minutes. Arrange the prawns on the sides of the wok, out of the oil, then add the ginger and garlic and stir until fragrant. Add the spring onion and chilli bean sauce. Stir the prawns into the mixture.

2 Reduce the heat slightly and add the rice wine, sugar, soy sauce and stock. Cover and cook for a further minute.

3 Remove the prawns with a slotted spoon and transfer to serving plates. Pour any remaining sauce into a small bowl. Serve the prawns immediately with the sauce on the side.

Prawn Cocktail

Serves 4

ingredients
- ½ Webbs lettuce, finely shredded
- 150 ml/5 fl oz mayonnaise (see page 22)
- 2 tbsp single cream
- 2 tbsp tomato ketchup
- a few drops of Tabasco sauce, or to taste
- juice of ½ lemon, or to taste
- 175 g/6 oz cooked peeled prawns
- salt and pepper

to garnish
- paprika, for sprinkling
- 4 cooked prawns, in their shells
- 4 lemon wedges

1 Divide the lettuce among small serving dishes.

2 Mix together the mayonnaise, cream and ketchup in a bowl. Add the Tabasco sauce and lemon juice, and season well with salt and pepper.

3 Divide the peeled prawns equally among the dishes and pour over the dressing. Cover and leave to chill in the refrigerator for 30 minutes.

4 Sprinkle a little paprika over the cocktails and garnish each dish with a prawn in its shell and a lemon wedge. Serve immediately.

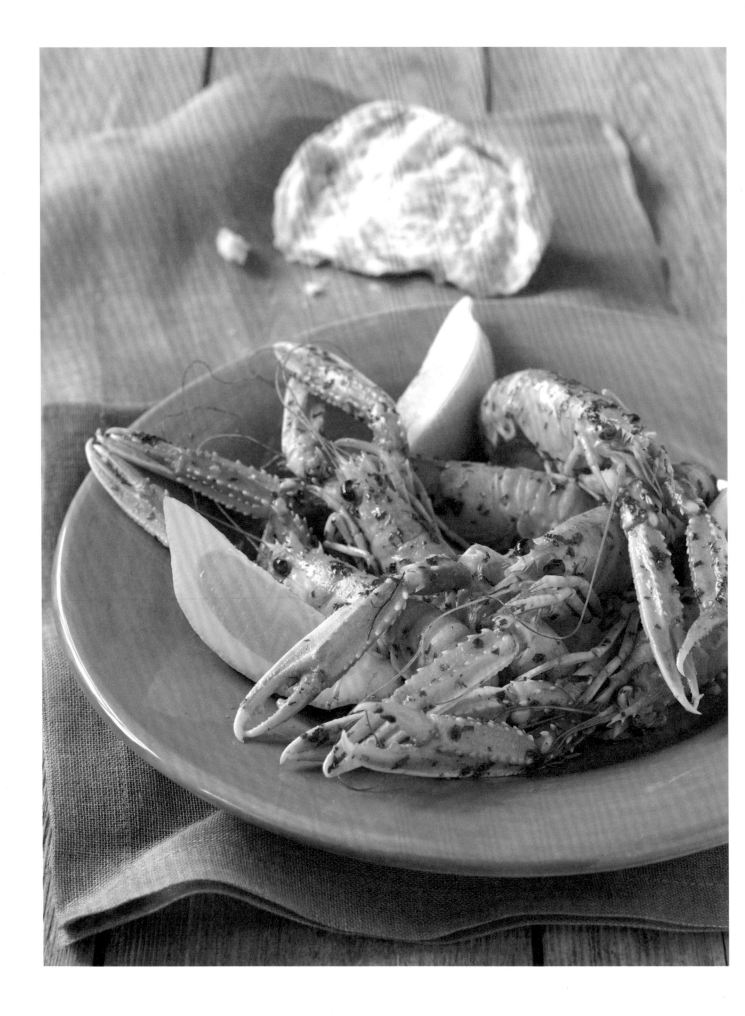

Garlic & Herb
Dublin Bay Prawns

Serves 2

ingredients
- juice of ½ lemon
- 2 garlic cloves, crushed
- 3 tbsp chopped fresh parsley
- 1 tbsp chopped fresh dill
- 40 g/1½ oz butter, softened
- 12 raw Dublin Bay prawns or langoustines
- salt and pepper
- lemon wedges and fresh crusty bread, to serve

1 Mix the lemon juice with the garlic, herbs and butter to form a paste. Season well with salt and pepper. Spread the paste over the prawns and leave to marinate for 30 minutes.

2 Preheat the grill to medium. Cook the prawns under the preheated grill for 5–6 minutes. Alternatively, heat a frying pan and fry the prawns in the paste until cooked.

3 Turn out onto warmed plates and pour over the pan juices. Serve immediately with lemon wedges for squeezing over and crusty bread for mopping up the juices.

Lobster Thermidor

Serves 2–4

ingredients

- 2 cooked lobsters, each about 750 g/1 lb 10 oz
- 55 g/2 oz butter
- 1 shallot, chopped
- 25 g/1 oz plain flour
- 300 ml/10 fl oz milk
- 1½ tsp chopped fresh chervil
- 1 tsp chopped fresh tarragon
- 1½ tsp chopped fresh flat-leaf parsley, plus extra sprigs to garnish
- 2 tsp Dijon mustard
- 6 tbsp dry white wine
- 3 tbsp double cream
- 4 tbsp grated Parmesan cheese
- salt and pepper
- lemon wedges, to garnish

1 Preheat the grill to high. Twist off and discard the lobster heads and pull off the claws. Crack the claws with a small hammer and remove the flesh. Using a sharp knife, split the lobsters in half lengthways and remove and discard the intestinal vein. Remove the flesh and reserve. Scrub the half shells under cold running water and drain upside down on kitchen paper. Cut the lobster flesh into 2 cm/¾ inch thick slices.

2 Melt the butter in a heavy-based saucepan. Add the shallot and cook over a low heat for 4–5 minutes, or until soft. Sprinkle in the flour and cook, stirring constantly, for 2 minutes. Remove the pan from the heat and gradually stir in the milk. Return the pan to the heat and bring to the boil, stirring. Cook, stirring, until thickened and smooth.

3 Reduce the heat, stir in the chopped herbs and the mustard and season to taste with salt and pepper. Remove the saucepan from the heat and whisk in the wine and cream. Return to a low heat and simmer until thickened. Add the lobster flesh and heat through for 2–3 minutes.

4 Divide the mixture among the lobster half shells and sprinkle with the Parmesan cheese. Cook under the preheated grill until the topping is golden and bubbling. Serve immediately, garnished with lemon wedges and parsley sprigs.

Stir-fried Fresh Crab
with Ginger

Serves 4

ingredients
- 3 tbsp vegetable or groundnut oil
- 2 large fresh crabs, cleaned, broken into pieces and legs cracked with a cleaver
- 55 g/2 oz fresh ginger, cut into julienne strips
- 100 g/3½ oz spring onions, cut into 5-cm/2-inch lengths
- 2 tbsp light soy sauce
- 1 tsp sugar
- pinch of white pepper

1 Preheat a wok or deep saucepan, then add 2 tablespoons of the oil and heat. Stir-fry the crab over a high heat for 3–4 minutes. Remove from the wok and set aside.

2 In a clean wok or deep saucepan, heat the remaining oil, add the ginger and stir until fragrant. Add the spring onions, then stir in the crab pieces. Add the soy sauce, sugar and pepper. Cover and simmer for 1 minute. Serve immediately.

Calamares

Serves 6

ingredients
- 450 g/1 lb prepared squid
- plain flour, for dusting
- sunflower oil, for deep-frying
- salt
- lemon wedges and aïoli (see page 22), to serve

1 Slice the squid into 1-cm/½-inch rings and halve the tentacles if large. Rinse under cold running water and pat dry with kitchen paper. Dust the squid rings with flour so that they are lightly coated.

2 Heat the oil in a deep-fat fryer or heavy-based saucepan to 180–190°C/350–375°F, or until a cube of bread browns in 30 seconds. Fry the squid rings, in batches, turning several times, for 2–3 minutes, or until golden brown and crisp all over. Do not overcook as the squid will become tough and rubbery rather than moist and tender.

3 Remove with a slotted spoon and drain well on kitchen paper. Keep warm while you fry the remaining squid rings.

4 Sprinkle the fried squid rings with salt and serve piping hot, accompanied by lemon wedges for squeezing over and aïoli for dipping.

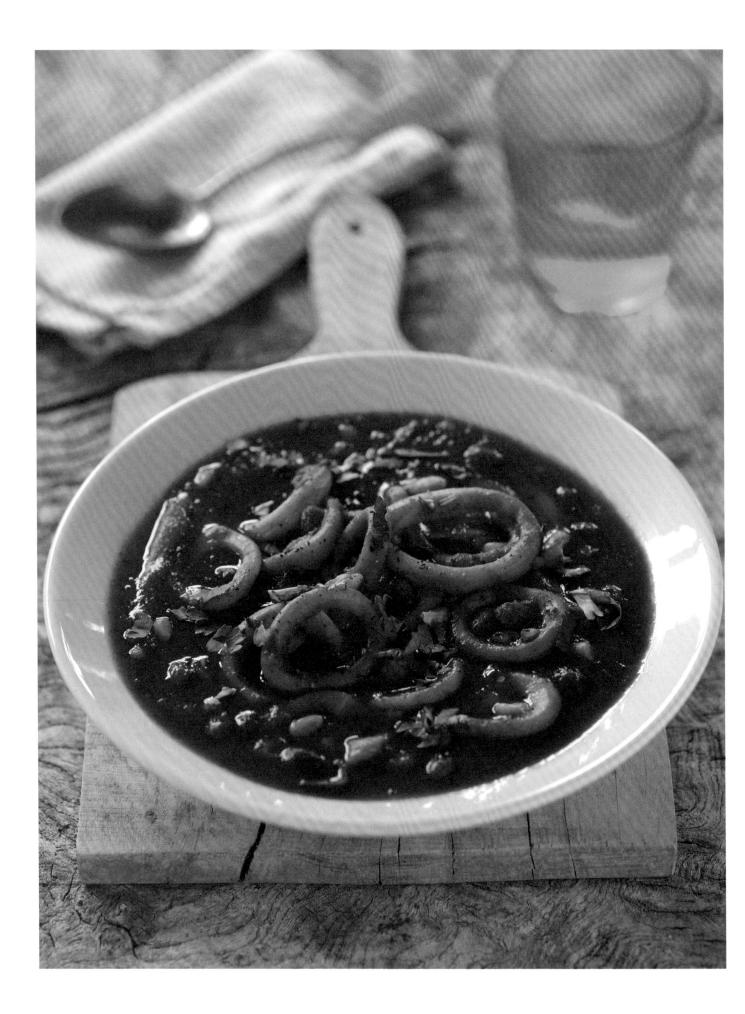

Squid with Parsley & Pine Kernels

Serves 4

ingredients
- 85 g/3 oz sultanas
- 5 tbsp olive oil
- 6 tbsp chopped fresh flat-leaf parsley, plus extra to garnish
- 2 garlic cloves, finely chopped
- 800 g/1 lb 12 oz prepared squid, sliced
- 125 ml/4 fl oz dry white wine
- 500 ml/18 fl oz passata
- pinch of chilli powder
- 85 g/3 oz pine kernels, roughly chopped
- salt

1 Place the sultanas in a small bowl, cover with lukewarm water and set aside for 15 minutes to plump up.

2 Meanwhile, heat the oil in a heavy-based saucepan. Add the parsley and garlic and cook over a low heat, stirring frequently, for 3 minutes. Add the squid and cook, stirring occasionally, for 5 minutes.

3 Increase the heat to medium, pour in the wine and cook until it has almost completely evaporated. Stir in the passata and season to taste with chilli powder and salt. Reduce the heat, cover and simmer gently, stirring occasionally, for 45–50 minutes, until the squid is almost tender.

4 Drain the sultanas and stir them into the pan with the pine kernels. Simmer for a further 10 minutes. Serve immediately, sprinkled with parsley.

Seafood Pasta Parcels

Serves 4

ingredients

- 1.5 kg/3 lb 5 oz freshly cooked crabmeat, shells reserved
- 450 g/1 lb live mussels, scrubbed and debearded
- 2 tbsp virgin olive oil
- 2 fresh red chillies, deseeded and finely chopped
- 4 garlic cloves, finely chopped
- 800 g/1 lb 12 oz canned chopped tomatoes
- 225 ml/8 fl oz dry white wine
- 350 g/12 oz dried spaghetti
- 25 g/1 oz butter
- 115 g/4 oz prepared squid, sliced
- 175 g/6 oz raw jumbo prawns, peeled and deveined
- 3 tbsp roughly chopped fresh flat-leaf parsley
- 1 tbsp shredded fresh basil leaves, plus extra sprigs to garnish
- salt and pepper

1 Carefully break up the larger pieces of crab shell with a meat mallet or the end of a rolling pin. Discard any mussels with broken shells and any that refuse to close when tapped.

2 Heat 1 tablespoon of the oil in a large saucepan. Add half the chillies and half the garlic, then add the pieces of crab shell. Cook over a medium heat, stirring occasionally, for 2–3 minutes. Add the tomatoes with their can juices and the wine. Reduce the heat and simmer for about 1 hour.

3 Strain the sauce, pressing down on the contents of the sieve with a wooden spoon. Season to taste with salt and pepper and set aside.

4 Bring a large saucepan of lightly salted water to the boil. Add the pasta, bring back to the boil and cook for 8–10 minutes, until the pasta is tender but still firm to the bite.

5 Preheat the oven to 180°C/350°F/Gas Mark 4.

6 Heat the remaining oil with the butter in a large heavy-based saucepan. Add the remaining chilli and garlic, and cook over a low heat, stirring occasionally, for 5 minutes, until soft. Add the squid, prawns and mussels, cover and cook over a high heat for 4–5 minutes, until the mussels have opened. Add the crabmeat and heat through for 2–3 minutes. Remove the saucepan from the heat and discard any mussels that remain closed.

7 Drain the pasta and add it to the seafood with the chilli and tomato sauce, the parsley and shredded basil, tossing well to coat.

8 Cut out four large squares of baking paper or greaseproof paper. Divide the pasta and seafood among them, placing it on one half of each square. Fold over the other half and turn in the edges securely to seal. Transfer to a large baking tray and bake in the preheated oven for about 10 minutes, until the parcels have puffed up. Serve immediately, garnished with basil sprigs.

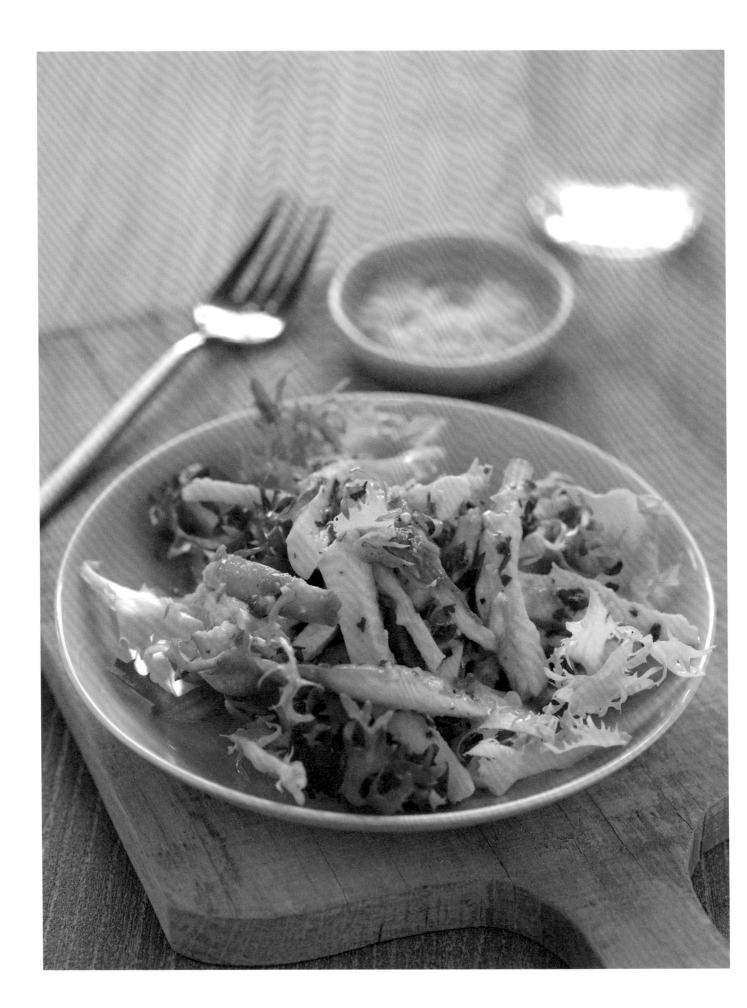

Octopus with Lemon & Chilli Dressing

Serves 4

ingredients

- 2 kg/4 lb 8 oz prepared octopus, cleaned and gutted
- 350–425 ml/12–15 fl oz olive oil
- juice and finely grated rind of 1 lemon
- 1–2 fresh green chillies, deseeded and finely chopped
- 1–2 garlic cloves, finely chopped
- 1 tbsp chopped fresh coriander
- salt and pepper
- salad leaves, to serve

1 Preheat the oven to 150°C/300°F/ Gas Mark 2.

2 Place the octopus in a lidded casserole just large enough to hold it and pour in enough of the oil to cover. Cover and cook in the preheated oven for 2 hours, until very tender.

3 Drain the octopus well and discard the cooking oil. Separate the tentacles and run your hand firmly along each one to remove the suckers. Thinly slice the tentacles and place in a bowl.

4 Mix together 125 ml/4 fl oz of the remaining oil, the lemon juice and rind, chilli, garlic and coriander in jug. Season to taste with salt and pepper and pour the dressing over the octopus. Toss gently, then cover with clingfilm and chill in the refrigerator for at least 2 hours. Serve with salad leaves.

Chapter 5
Preserved Fish

Ways to Preserve Fish

In the days before modern refrigeration and transportation fish preservation was necessary to prevent spoilage and ensure year-round supplies. That isn't the case any longer, but canned, dried, frozen, pickled, salted and smoked fish remain popular because of their unique flavours, versatility and convenience.

Cans of goodness

Cans of anchovy fillets, clams, mussels, oysters, salmon, mackerel, shrimp and sardines are handy staples in every kitchen to add flavour to quick sandwich fillings, pasta sauces and baked suppers.

The canning process, which gives fish long shelf lives of several years, preserves many of the seafood's vitamins and minerals, but you should, however, always note the best-before dates.

Canned tuna is available preserved in brine, oil and spring water for variety, and you'll also find sardines canned in tomato sauce and oil.

Dried and salted for long life

Both air-drying and salting are ancient techniques for removing moisture from fresh fish, delaying spoilage for varying lengths of time. One of the most fascinating transformations in the culinary world is how a piece of dried salt cod that looks like dry cardboard is transformed into tender, flaky fish by lengthy soaking in water. Especially popular in Mediterranean and Scandinavian countries, salt cod, also called *stockfish* in Scandinavia, *morue* in France, *baccala* in Italy and *bacalhau* in Portugal, was once an essential winter staple, but today its appeal is its flavour. It remains a popular ingredient in dishes such as fish cakes or creamed salt cod. It is usually sold in long, dried fillets. Try to buy middle slices, as they will cook most evenly.

Caviar is salted sturgeon roe, although less expensive salted lumpfish and salmon roes are also available as are dried cod and grey mullet roes. A dry mixture of salt, peppercorns and dill are rubbed on salmon fillets to make gravadlax, a Scandinavian favourite.

Frozen or fresh?

Although it might sound like a contradiction in terms, frozen fish is often fresher than the fish you buy at the fishmongers. Large commercial fishing vessels are capable of processing and freezing the catch within hours of it coming out of the water, which keeps it in prime condition. If you follow the instructions on the packaging, fish steaks and fillets can be cooked from frozen.

In a pickle

Pickling is an old-fashioned form of preserving that remains popular because the sweet-sour taste of the flavoured vinegar, or brine, enhances the taste of the fish. Oily fish, because of the natural oils they contain, are well suited to this process. Rollmops, pickled herring rolled around onions and spices, for example, have travelled from Scandinavia to tables around the globe.

In hot climates, such as South America, the Mediterranean and Mexico, fresh white fish and shellfish are left to marinate in lemon or lime juice with herbs for a quick form of pickling that is intended for immediate consumption. The acid in the juice 'cooks' the flesh, making it safe for human consumption.

Simply smoked

Smoked salmon is perhaps the best-known smoked fish, but many other species are also successfully smoked. Oily fish, such as herring and mackerel, are ideal, and haddock, trout and shellfish are also popular. (Cans of smoked mussels and oysters are useful for making impromptu nibbles to enjoy with drinks.)

Scottish smoked haddock, such as finnan haddock and Arbroath smokies, for example, like a myriad of other examples, is enjoyed around the world in soups, rich pâtés and mousses and as breakfast dishes.

Fish is either cold-smoked or hot-smoked. Cold-smoked fish is first brined or salted before being left to hang over a slow-burning fire. Although all producers follow the same basic technique that has been used for generations, they stamp their individual mark on the final product by using different-flavoured brine and different wood chips for the smoke. If possible, always taste before you buy.

Some cold-smoked fish is ready to eat, while others will require cooking. When a fish is hot-smoked, however, it is given an initial blast of hot air at the beginning of the process before slow smoking, so it is ready to eat, making it a very healthy type of fast food.

Preparing Sushi

Sushi originated centuries ago as a way of extending the shelf life of dried fish by placing it between layers of vinegared rice. The word sushi actually refers to the vinegared rice, but its meaning has now been extended to describe a finger-sized piece of raw fish or seafood on a bed of cold vinegared rice.

Equipment needed

Very little specialized equipment is required, although you can buy sushi-making kits in various outlets, including larger supermarkets. The key to the technique is a bamboo sushi mat with which to make the most common form, rolled sushi.

A kit may include a special mixing tub, a pressing box and a spatula.

Which fish?

Meatier types of round fish, such as cod, tuna, salmon, trout, mackerel and eel, are all suitable for sushi, as are prawns, lobster, squid, scallops, crab and fish roe. Smoked versions of haddock, salmon, trout and mackerel are also popular. Many sushi recipes use raw fish. Always buy it from a reliable supplier who offers 'sushi' or 'sashimi grade' fish, which is as fresh as possible, because raw fish contains more bacteria and parasites than cooked fish. Similarly, look for shellfish from certified waters. Only buy fish or shellfish on the day you

intend to eat it and keep it refrigerated. Ensure that the fish is prepared using clean utensils.

Preparing sushi rice

Sushi is a short-grained rice, and several brands are available. The hot cooked rice is tipped into a large, shallow dish and sushi rice seasoning spread over the surface. With one hand you mix in the seasoning with a spatula; with the other you fan the rice to cool it quickly. The finished rice should have a shiny appearance and be at room temperature.

Presenting sushi

Presentation is all, and the best sushi are minor works of culinary art. You need to have all the ingredients assembled, the rice cooled and the garnishes, pickles or dipping sauces prepared so that you can serve the sushi immediately.

Scattered sushi

This is where sushi rice is mixed loosely with other ingredients, and is very easy to make. It is often served as an attractive individual bowl for each person.

Boat sushi

These dishes are prepared by wrapping nori around rice moulded into oval shapes. Using nori is an ideal way to serve sushi with fish roe or soft toppings that would otherwise be messy to handle.

Pressed sushi

This type is made by pressing the rice into a special three-piece bamboo box, although you can improvise using a loose-based tin or terrine tin with drop-down sides. If you have a fixed-base tin, the sushi has to be made upside down, and the sushi turned out after the flavours have had time to mix and develop.

Rolled sushi

These are best made using a sushi mat, available from kitchen shops and some supermarkets.

A sheet of nori (dried seaweed), is placed on the bamboo mat and the filling heaped along the bottom third of the nori.

By folding the mat over the filling, then lifting the mat and keeping an even pressure along the length, the roll is formed. It is cut, using a very sharp, wet knife, into rounds, which are then placed on one end to present the filling.

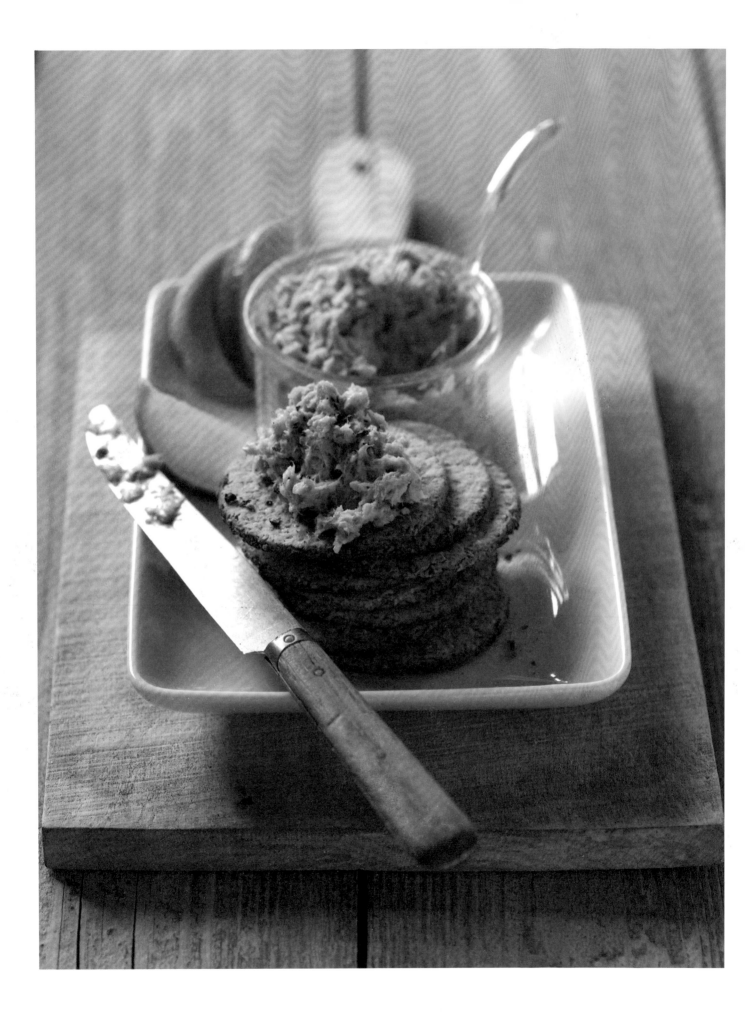

Smoked Fish Pâté

Serves 8

ingredients
- 900 g/2 lb undyed kipper fillets
- 2 garlic cloves, finely chopped
- 175 ml/6 fl oz olive oil
- 6 tbsp single cream
- salt and pepper
- lemon and lime slices, to garnish
- oatcakes, to serve

1 Put the kippers in a large frying pan or fish kettle and add cold water to just cover. Bring to the boil, then immediately reduce the heat and poach gently for 10 minutes, until tender. If using a frying pan, you may need to do this in batches.

2 Transfer the fish to a chopping board using a fish slice. Remove and discard the skin. Roughly flake the flesh with a fork and remove and discard any remaining tiny bones. Transfer the fish to a saucepan over a low heat, add the garlic and break up the fish with a wooden spoon.

3 Gradually add the oil, beating well after each addition. Add the cream and beat until smooth, but do not allow the mixture to boil.

4 Remove the saucepan from the heat and season to taste with salt, if needed, and pepper. Spoon the pâté into a serving dish, cover and set aside to cool completely. Chill in the refrigerator until required, for up to 3 days.

5 Garnish with lemon and lime slices and serve with oatcakes.

Smoked Cod Chowder

Serves 4

ingredients
- 350 g/12 oz smoked cod fillets, skinned
- 25 g/1 oz butter
- 1 onion, finely chopped
- 1 small celery stick, finely diced
- 250 g/9 oz potatoes, diced
- 55 g/2 oz carrots, diced
- 300 ml/10 fl oz boiling water
- 300 ml/10 fl oz milk
- salt and pepper
- fresh flat-leaf parsley sprigs, to garnish
- fresh crusty bread, to serve

1 Rinse the fish under cold running water and pat dry with kitchen paper. Cut the fish into bite-sized chunks.

2 Melt the butter in a large saucepan over a low heat, add the onion and celery, and cook, stirring frequently, for 5 minutes, or until soft but not brown.

3 Add the potatoes, carrots, water, and salt and pepper to taste. Bring to the boil, then reduce the heat and simmer for 10 minutes, or until the vegetables are tender. Add the fish to the chowder and cook for a further 10 minutes.

4 Pour in the milk and heat gently. Taste and adjust the seasoning, adding salt and pepper if needed. Ladle into warmed soup bowls, garnish with parsley sprigs and serve immediately with crusty bread.

Kedgeree

Serves 4

ingredients
- 450 g/1 lb undyed smoked haddock, skinned
- 2 tbsp olive oil
- 1 onion, finely chopped
- 1 tsp mild curry paste
- 175 g/6 oz long-grain white rice
- 55 g/2 oz butter
- 3 hard-boiled eggs
- salt and pepper
- 2 tbsp chopped fresh parsley, to garnish

1 Rinse the fish under cold running water and pat dry with kitchen paper. Put the fish in a large saucepan and cover with water. Bring the water to the boil, then reduce the heat and simmer for 8–10 minutes, until the fish flakes easily.

2 Remove the fish with a slotted spoon and keep warm, reserving the cooking liquid in a jug or bowl.

3 Heat the oil in the pan over a medium heat, add the onion and cook, stirring frequently, for 4 minutes, or until soft. Stir in the curry paste and add the rice.

4 Measure 600 ml/1 pint of the haddock cooking liquid and return to the pan. Bring to a simmer and cover. Cook for 10–12 minutes, until the rice is tender and the water has been absorbed. Season to taste with salt and pepper.

5 Flake the fish and add to the pan with the butter. Stir very gently over a low heat until the butter has melted. Chop two of the hard-boiled eggs and add to the pan.

6 Turn the kedgeree into a serving dish, slice the remaining hard-boiled egg and use to garnish. Scatter over the parsley and serve immediately.

Smoked Salmon Risotto

Serves 4

ingredients
- 1.2 litres/2 pints vegetable stock
- ½ small fennel bulb
- 50 g/1¾ oz butter
- 1 small onion, finely chopped
- 500 g/1 lb 2 oz risotto rice
- 300 ml/10 fl oz dry white wine or vermouth
- 150 g/5½ oz hot smoked salmon flakes
- 150 g/5½ oz smoked salmon slices
- salt and pepper

1 Bring the stock to the boil in a saucepan, then reduce the heat and keep simmering gently over a low heat while you are cooking the risotto.

2 Trim the fennel, reserving the fronds for garnish, and finely chop the flesh.

3 Melt half the butter in a deep saucepan over a medium heat. Add the onion and fennel and cook, stirring occasionally, for 5–8 minutes, until soft and translucent.

4 Reduce the heat, add the rice and mix to coat in butter. Cook, stirring constantly, for 2–3 minutes, or until the grains are translucent. Pour in the wine and cook, stirring constantly, for 1 minute, until reduced.

5 Gradually add the hot stock, a ladleful at a time. Stir constantly and add more liquid as the rice absorbs each addition. Cook for 20 minutes, or until all the liquid is absorbed and the rice is creamy but still firm to the bite.

6 Remove the risotto from the heat and stir in the remaining butter and the two types of salmon. Season to taste with salt and pepper. Spoon the risotto onto warmed plates, garnish with the reserved fennel fronds and serve immediately.

Smoked Trout Salad
with Pears

Serves 4

ingredients

- 55 g/2 oz watercress
- 1 head of radicchio, torn into pieces
- 4 smoked trout fillets, skinned
- 2 ripe pears
- 6 tsp lemon juice
- 2 tbsp extra virgin olive oil
- 3 tbsp soured cream
- 2 tsp creamed horseradish
- salt and pepper
- thin slices of buttered brown bread, crusts removed, to serve

1 Place the watercress and radicchio in a bowl. Cut the trout fillets into thin strips and add to the bowl. Halve and core the pears, then slice thinly. Place in a separate bowl, add 4 teaspoons of the lemon juice and toss to coat. Add the pears to the salad.

2 To make the dressing, mix the remaining lemon juice and the oil together in a bowl, then season to taste with salt and pepper. Pour the dressing over the salad and toss well. Transfer to a large salad bowl.

3 Mix the soured cream and horseradish together in a separate bowl until thoroughly blended. Transfer to a small serving bowl.

4 Divide the salad among serving plates. Serve immediately, accompanied by the soured cream mixture and buttered bread.

Caribbean Crab Cakes

Serves 4

ingredients
- 1 floury potato, peeled and cut into chunks
- pinch of salt
- 4 spring onions, chopped
- 1 garlic clove, chopped
- 1 tbsp chopped fresh thyme
- 1 tbsp chopped fresh basil
- 1 tbsp chopped fresh coriander
- 225 g/8 oz canned white crabmeat, drained
- ½ tsp Dijon mustard
- ½ fresh green chilli, deseeded and finely chopped
- 1 egg, lightly beaten
- plain flour, for dusting
- sunflower oil, for shallow-frying
- pepper
- lime wedges, to garnish
- salsa, to serve

1 Put the potato in a small saucepan, add water to cover and the salt. Bring to the boil, then reduce the heat, cover and simmer for 10–15 minutes, until soft. Drain well, turn into a large bowl and mash with a potato masher or fork until smooth.

2 Meanwhile, put the spring onions, garlic, thyme, basil and coriander in a mortar and pound with a pestle until smooth.

3 Add the herb paste to the mashed potato with the crabmeat, mustard, chilli, egg and pepper to taste. Mix well, cover with clingfilm and chill in the refrigerator for 30 minutes.

4 Sprinkle flour onto a large plate. Shape spoonfuls of the crabmeat mixture into small balls with your hands, then flatten slightly and dust with flour, shaking off any excess.

5 Heat enough oil for shallow-frying in a frying pan over a high heat, add the crab cakes and cook, in batches, for 2–3 minutes on each side, until golden. Remove with a slotted spoon and drain on kitchen paper. Set aside to cool to room temperature.

6 Arrange the crab cakes on a serving plate, garnish with lime wedges and serve with a bowl of salsa.

Tuna Noodle Casserole

Serves 4

ingredients
- 200 g/7 oz dried ribbon pasta, such as tagliatelle
- 25 g/1 oz butter
- 55 g/2 oz fine fresh breadcrumbs
- 400 ml/14 fl oz canned condensed cream of mushroom soup
- 125 ml/4 fl oz milk
- 2 celery sticks, chopped
- 1 red and 1 green pepper, deseeded and chopped
- 140 g/5 oz mature Cheddar cheese, coarsely grated
- 2 tbsp chopped fresh flat-leaf parsley, plus extra sprigs to garnish
- 200 g/7 oz canned tuna in oil, drained and flaked
- salt and pepper

1 Preheat the oven to 200°C/400°F/Gas Mark 6. Bring a large saucepan of lightly salted water to the boil. Add the pasta, bring back to the boil and cook for 2 minutes fewer than specified on the packet instructions.

2 Meanwhile, melt the butter in a small saucepan over a medium heat. Stir in the breadcrumbs, then remove from the heat and reserve.

3 Drain the pasta well and reserve. Pour the soup into the pasta pan and place over a medium heat, then stir in the milk, celery, peppers, half the cheese and the chopped parsley. Add the tuna and gently stir in so that the flakes don't break up. Season to taste with salt and pepper. Heat just until small bubbles appear around the edge of the mixture – do not boil.

4 Stir the pasta into the pan and use two forks to mix all the ingredients together. Spoon the mixture into an ovenproof dish and spread out.

5 Stir the remaining cheese into the buttered breadcrumbs, then sprinkle over the top of the pasta mixture. Bake in the preheated oven for 20–25 minutes, until the topping is golden. Leave to stand for 5 minutes. Spoon onto warmed plates and serve immediately, garnished with parsley sprigs.

Creamed Salt Cod

Serves 4–6

ingredients
- 700 g/1 lb 9 oz salt cod
- 300 ml/10 fl oz olive oil
- 2 large garlic cloves, very finely chopped
- 300 ml/10 fl oz single cream
- lemon juice, to taste
- pepper
- chopped stoned black olives and chopped fresh flat-leaf parsley, to garnish
- fried croûtes, to serve

1 Cut or break the salt cod into pieces that will fit in a large bowl of water, then leave to soak for up to 48 hours, replacing the water with fresh water about every 8 hours to remove the saltiness.

2 Drain the salt cod, then transfer it to a saucepan and cover with fresh water. Slowly bring to a simmer and leave to simmer for 15–20 minutes, until it is tender and flakes easily.

3 Meanwhile, heat the oil in a heavy-based saucepan until the surface shimmers. Add the garlic and set aside to infuse.

4 Drain the salt cod. When it is cool enough to handle, remove all the skin and small bones, then flake the flesh into a food processor.

5 Reheat the garlic-infused oil and heat the cream in a separate saucepan. With the food processor's motor running, add about 2 tablespoons of the oil, then 2 tablespoons of the cream to the cod. Continue adding the oil and cream until they are absorbed and the cod has the consistency of mashed potatoes.

6 Taste the mixture and add lemon juice and pepper to taste. Spoon the salt cod mixture into a serving bowl and garnish with olives and parsley. Serve with fried croûtes.

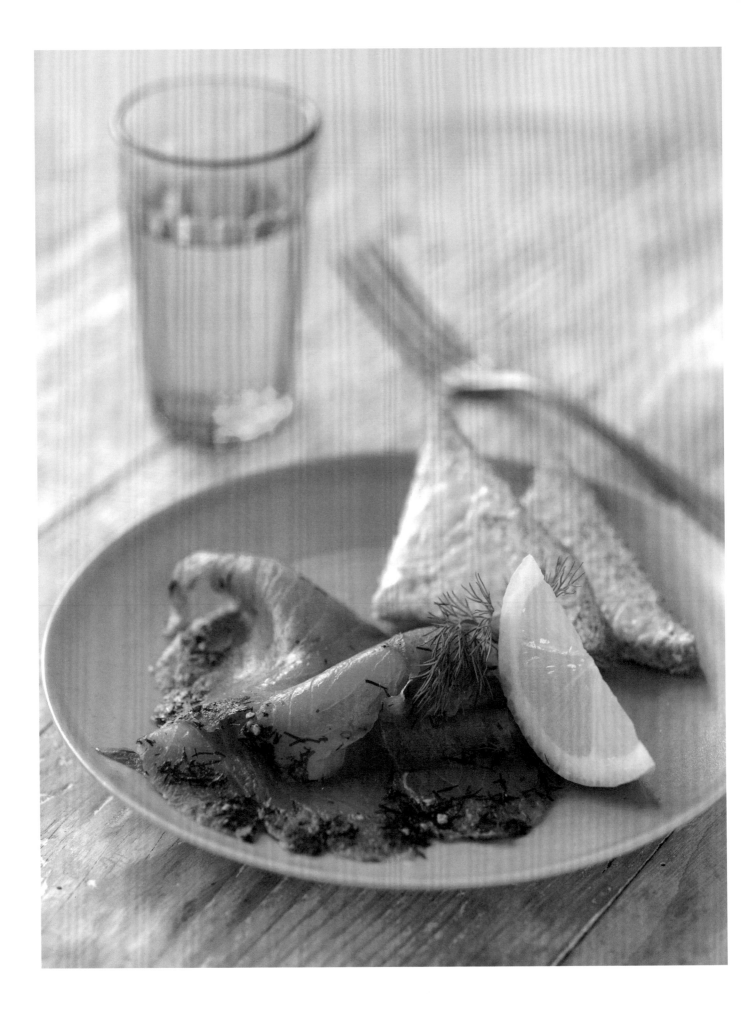

Gravadlax

Serves 8–12

ingredients

- 2 salmon fillets, skin on, each about 450 g/1 lb
- 6 tbsp roughly chopped fresh dill, plus extra sprigs to garnish
- 115 g/4 oz sea salt
- 50 g/1¾ oz sugar
- 1 tbsp white peppercorns, roughly crushed
- lemon wedges, to garnish
- thin slices of buttered brown bread, to serve

1 Rinse the salmon fillets under cold running water and pat dry with kitchen paper. Put one fillet, skin-side down, in a non-metallic dish.

2 Mix together the chopped dill, sea salt, sugar and peppercorns in a small bowl. Spread this mixture over the fillet in the dish and put the second fillet, skin-side up, on top. Put a plate, the same size as the fish, on top and weigh down with 3–4 food cans.

3 Chill in the refrigerator for 2 days, turning the fish about every 12 hours and basting with any juices that come out of the fish.

4 Remove the salmon from the brine and thinly slice, without slicing the skin, as you would smoked salmon. Garnish with the lemon wedges and dill sprigs, and serve with buttered bread.

Ceviche

Serves 6

ingredients

- 600 g/1 lb 5 oz fish fillets –
  mix three different types from
  salmon, sea bass, scallops,
  trout, monkfish, tuna, lemon sole,
  halibut or super-fresh pollack (ask
  your fishmonger to fillet and skin
  them, if possible)
- grated rind of 1 lime
- juice of 2 limes
- juice of 2 lemons
- juice of 1 orange
- 1 fresh red chilli, deseeded and
  finely sliced
- dash of Tabasco sauce
- 2 tbsp extra virgin olive oil, plus
  extra for drizzling
- ½ tsp sugar
- ½ shallot or small onion, finely
  sliced
- 1 tbsp roughly chopped fresh
  coriander

1 Rinse the fish under cold running water and pat dry with kitchen paper. Skin the fish, if not already done, then carefully remove any pin-bones that run down the middle. You can use pliers or fish tweezers for this, but take your time because the fish must be bone-free. Cut the fillets into sashimi-thick slices across the grain – about ½ cm/¼ inch thick.

2 In a large non-metallic bowl, mix together all the remaining ingredients, except the coriander. Add the fish and toss well to coat. Place in the refrigerator for about 1 hour – you can leave it for a little longer if you want it a little more 'cooked', but no more than 2 hours or it will be overdone.

3 Mix in the coriander and transfer the fish to serving plates with a few spoonfuls of the juices. Drizzle with a little extra virgin olive oil and serve.

Scattered Sushi with Smoked Mackerel

Serves 4

ingredients
- 8 mangetout
- 5-cm/2-inch piece mooli
- 1 quantity freshly cooked sushi rice (see page 22)
- juice and finely grated rind of 1 lemon
- 2 spring onions, finely chopped
- 2 smoked mackerel fillets, skinned and cut into diagonal strips
- ½ cucumber, peeled and cut into slices

to garnish
- pickled ginger
- strips of toasted nori
- wasabi paste

1 Bring a saucepan of lightly salted water to the boil, add the mangetout and blanch for 1 minute. Drain and set aside to cool.

2 Shred the mooli using the finest setting on a mandolin or a very sharp knife. If you are using a knife, cut the mooli into long, thin slices and cut each slice along its length as finely as you can.

3 Mix the sushi rice with the lemon juice and rind.

4 Divide the rice among small serving bowls – they should be filled to a depth of about 2 cm/¾ inch. Scatter the spring onions over the top. Arrange the mackerel, cucumber, mangetout and mooli on top of the rice. Garnish with pickled ginger, nori strips and a little wasabi paste.

Pressed Sushi Bars
with Smoked Salmon

Makes 8–10

ingredients
- vegetable oil, for oiling
- ½ quantity freshly cooked sushi rice (see page 22)
- 2 tbsp Japanese mayonnaise
- 200 g/7 oz smoked salmon
- ½ cucumber, peeled and cut into very thin slices
- lemon wedges and fresh mint sprigs, to garnish

1 Oil an oshi waku or terrine tin (preferably with drop-down sides) and line it with a piece of clingfilm so that the clingfilm hangs over the edges. Pack the tin 3 cm/1¼ inches deep with the sushi rice.

2 Spread a layer of mayonnaise on top of the rice. Arrange the smoked salmon and cucumber in diagonal strips on top of the rice, doubling up the smoked salmon layers if you have enough so that the topping is quite thick.

3 Cover the top of the rice with a strip of clingfilm, put another terrine tin on top of the clingfilm and weigh down with a couple of food cans.

4 Chill the sushi in the refrigerator for 15 minutes. Remove the cans and the top tin, then lift out the sushi and discard the clingfilm. Cut the sushi into 8–10 pieces with a very sharp, wet knife. Garnish with lemon wedges and mint sprigs before serving.

Smoked Trout Sushi Boats

Makes 8

ingredients
- ⅓ quantity freshly cooked sushi rice (see page 22)
- 2 small sheets of toasted nori, each cut into 4 strips lengthways
- 2 tbsp Japanese mayonnaise
- 1 tsp grated lemon rind
- 2 tsp lemon juice
- 2 spring onions, finely chopped
- 1 smoked trout fillet, flaked
- 55 g/2 oz smoked salmon, cut into strips
- ponzu sauce and finely chopped radishes, to serve

1 Divide the sushi rice into 8 batches. Dampen your hands to prevent the rice from sticking, then shape each batch of the rice into an oval using your hands.

2 Carefully wrap a strip of nori around each piece of rice, trim off any excess, then stick together at the join using a couple of crushed grains of rice.

3 Mix the mayonnaise with the lemon rind and juice, and spread a little on top of each sushi boat. Sprinkle each with some spring onion, then top with some of the smoked trout and smoked salmon. Serve the sushi immediately with ponzu sauce and radishes.

Conversion Charts

temperatures

CELSIUS (°C)	GAS MARK	FAHRENHEIT (°F)
110	$\frac{1}{4}$	225
120	$\frac{1}{2}$	250
140	1	275
150	2	300
160	3	325
180	4	350
190	5	375
200	6	400
220	7	425
230	8	450
240	9	475

volume measures

METRIC	IMPERIAL
1.25 ML	$\frac{1}{4}$ TSP
2.5 ML	$\frac{1}{2}$ TSP
5 ML	1 TSP
10 ML	2 TSP
15 ML	1 TBSP/3 TSP
30 ML	2 TBSP
45 ML	3 TBSP
60 ML	4 TBSP
75 ML	5 TBSP
90 ML	6 TBSP
15 ML	$\frac{1}{2}$ FL OZ
30 ML	1 FL OZ
50 ML	2 FL OZ
75 ML	$2\frac{1}{2}$ FL OZ
100 ML	$3\frac{1}{2}$ FL OZ
125 ML	4 FL OZ
150 ML	5 FL OZ
175 ML	6 FL OZ
200 ML	7 FL OZ
225 ML	8 FL OZ
250 ML	9 FL OZ
300 ML	10 FL OZ
350 ML	12 FL OZ
400 ML	14 FL OZ
425 ML	15 FL OZ
450 ML	16 FL OZ
500 ML	18 FL OZ
600 ML	1 PINT

weight measures

METRIC	IMPERIAL
5 G	$\frac{1}{8}$ OZ
10 G	$\frac{1}{4}$ OZ
15 G	$\frac{1}{2}$ OZ
25/30 G	1 OZ
35 G	$1\frac{1}{4}$ OZ
40 G	$1\frac{1}{2}$ OZ
50 G	$1\frac{3}{4}$ OZ
55 G	2 OZ
60 G	$2\frac{1}{4}$ OZ
70 G	$2\frac{1}{2}$ OZ
85 G	3 OZ
90 G	$3\frac{1}{4}$ OZ
100 G	$3\frac{1}{2}$ OZ
115 G	4 OZ
125 G	$4\frac{1}{2}$ OZ
140 G	5 OZ
150 G	$5\frac{1}{2}$ OZ
175 G	6 OZ
200 G	7 OZ
225 G	8 OZ
250 G	9 OZ
275 G	$9\frac{3}{4}$ OZ
280 G	10 OZ
300 G	$10\frac{1}{2}$ OZ
325 G	$11\frac{1}{2}$ OZ
350 G	12 OZ
375 G	13 OZ
400 G	14 OZ
425 G	15 OZ
450 G	1 LB
500 G	1 LB 2 OZ